T H E   B O O K   O F

Chocolate

THE BOOK OF

Chocolate

EDITED BY CAROL TENNANT

HPBooks

ANOTHER BEST SELLING VOLUME FROM HPBOOKS

HPBooks
Published by the Berkley Publishing Group
A division of Penguin Group (USA) Inc.
375 Hudson Street
New York, NY 10014

Editor: Carol Tennant
Designer: Cara Hamilton
Production: Don Campaniello
Filmset and reproduction by: Anorax Imaging Ltd

Visit our website at www.penguin.com

ISBN 1-55788-430-7

Printed and bound in Spain

10 9 8 7 6 5 4 3 2 1

Warning: It is possible that raw eggs may
contain salmonella. They should never be served
to very young children or anyone with a serious
illness or compromised immune system.
Pasteurized eggs are available in some markets
and can be used safely without cooking.

CONTENTS

INTRODUCTION

TYPES OF CHOCOLATE

When cooking with chocolate it is worth buying the best-quality chocolate that you can afford as it will show in the texture, flavor, and appearance of the finished dish. Look for chocolate with a high percentage of cocoa butter. It should contain a minimum of 34%—the best chocolate contains 50% or more—so check on the package.

Bitter chocolate or "baker's chocolate": this is unsweetened chocolate for cooking. It is not widely available, but is excellent used in baking.

Semisweet chocolate: the most useful type for cooking, as it gives a good strong chocolate flavor. However, quality varies considerably according to the proportion of cocoa solids listed in the ingredients. Good-quality chocolate is now readily available in supermarkets.

Milk chocolate: this type of chocolate is not satisfactory for use in cooking but once melted it may be piped onto semisweet chocolate in order to create a decorative effect.

White Chocolate: this is not really chocolate at all, as it comprises cocoa butter, milk, and sugar, but contains no chocolate liquor. It is not normally used for cooking because of its lack of flavor, but its creamy texture makes it suitable for use in cold desserts such as mousses, and it gives an interesting contrast when combined with semisweet chocolate.

Couverture: generally only available to professional confectioners. It has a high cocoa butter content and flows very smoothly, making it ideal for coating purposes. It must be tempered, by cooling very carefully to 79F (26C), before use.

Chocolate-flavored coating: contains a minimum of 2.5% cocoa solids, and vegetable oil instead of added

From top: Semisweet chocolate; milk chocolate; white chocolate; couverture; chocolate-flavor cake covering.

cocoa butter, which makes it considerably cheaper than "real" chocolate. For most purposes the flavor and texture are inferior, and not recommended for use in this collection of recipes.

Unsweetened cocoa: this is a convenient and inexpensive way of achieving a strong chocolate flavor in baking, but it is not suitable for use in uncooked dishes. A good substitute for bitter chocolate is a mixture of 9 teaspoons unsweetened cocoa and 3 teaspoons butter. Add 3 teaspoons sugar to provide a substitute for semisweet chocolate.

Hot chocolate mix: this is a mixture of cocoa and sugar. It is too sweet for use in cooking unless the sugar in the recipe is reduced accordingly.

From top: Unsweetened cocoa; drinking chocolate.

CAROB—THE ALTERNATIVE TO CHOCOLATE

Although processed carob and chocolate look similar, they are not related in any way. Carob is not chocolate at all, but a member of the legume family. Carob has been very popular with health food enthusiasts for some years, because it is rich in vitamins, contains no refined sugar, theobromine, caffeine, or oxalic acid and contains fewer calories weight for weight than chocolate. It is available as a powder or in bars, some of which have added flavorings or nuts. Carob can be substituted for chocolate in many recipes, although when melted it will not have the same shiny finish. It is pleasant used in cooking, with a mild chocolate flavor and pale color. However, for the chocolate lover and connoisseur, there is no substitute for the real thing!

STORING CHOCOLATE

Semisweet and milk chocolate have a shelf life of about one year, but white chocolate tends to deteriorate after about eight months. It should be well wrapped and stored in a cool place, but not the refrigerator. Chocolate stored at below 55°F (13°C) will develop a "bloom," and "sweat" when transferred to room temperature. Chocolate stored above 70°F (21°C) will also develop a "bloom."

"Bloom" is a grayish-white coating that appears on the surface of the chocolate. It affects the appearance but does not impair the flavor. It is not an indication that the chocolate has "gone off." "Fat bloom" is caused by heating and cooling chocolate. It is quite greasy and can easily be rubbed off. "Sugar bloom" shows as a white crust of sugar crystals on chocolate that has been stored in a refrigerator. It cannot be removed.

MELTING CHOCOLATE

Great care must be taken when melting chocolate, because it scorches very easily if overheated and will "seize" into hard, grainy lumps. This will also happen if any liquid or steam comes into contact with the chocolate while it is melting.

Chocolate can be safely melted with a small amount of liquid if they are placed in the bowl together. It will melt more evenly and quickly if the chocolate is broken or cut into small, even-sized pieces. Do not stir

In a plastic bag: this is a convenient way of melting a small quantity of chocolate, particularly if it is required for piped decorations. Place small, even-sized pieces of chocolate in a heavy-gauge plastic bag, seal, and stand the bag in hot, not boiling water. When the chocolate has melted, cut a corner off the bag, and use as required.

the chocolate until it has melted, and then stir it very gently. If the chocolate does seize, adding a small amount of oil to the chocolate can sometimes restore it.

Chocolate can be added to a large quantity of hot liquid and left to melt, without stirring. Stir it gently, when completely melted, to make a smooth mixture. White chocolate is particularly sensitive to heat, so extra care is needed when melting. There are several methods of melting chocolate successfully.

Over hot water: break the chocolate into small, even-sized pieces and place in a heatproof bowl set over a saucepan of simmering water. The bottom of the bowl must not touch the water. Remove the saucepan from the heat and let stand until the chocolate has melted.

In the oven: preheat the oven to 225°F (110°C). Break the chocolate into small squares or even-sized pieces and place in a shallow dish. Place in the oven and leave until the chocolate is soft.

In a microwave: this is a very successful way of melting chocolate. Break the chocolate into small, even-sized pieces and place in a microwave-proof bowl. Heat for 2 minutes on full power, stirring occasionally. The exact time needed depends on the quantity of chocolate, the size of bowl, and the wattage the of oven. When melting white chocolate in the microwave, set the oven on 50% power and use it in 1–2 minute bursts, stirring the chocolate at each interval.

USING MELTED CHOCOLATE

There are a few hints to enable you to use melted chocolate successfully.
• Let melted chocolate cool slightly before combining with other ingredients.
• You can add small quantities of butter or oil to make the chocolate smoother and more fluid for coating and dipping.
• Add the melted chocolate to other liquid ingredients, rather than pouring other liquids into the chocolate.
• When using melted chocolate in cake batters, add it after creaming the fat and sugar together and before adding the eggs and flour.
• For soufflé and mousse mixtures, combine the melted chocolate with the egg yolks and flavoring before adding the cream and egg whites.

MAKING CHOCOLATE DECORATIONS

Homemade chocolate decorations give a professional finish to a wide variety of cakes and desserts. With little practice, it is possible to produce an endless range of simple and elaborate decorations. Until you become more confident, experiment with chocolate coating because it is easier to work with and any disasters can be remelted and used again. Let the decorations set in a cool place before using, but do not place them in a refrigerator, otherwise they will develop an unattractive "bloom" (page 7).

Grated chocolate: one of the most effective chocolate decorations, and the simplest. Different effects can be achieved according to how coarsely the chocolate is grated. The grated chocolate can be sprinkled over a wide range of desserts and ices for a simple finish, or used to cover the top and sides of a cake, which has been coated with cream. For an attractive gâteau or cheesecake topping, alternate bands of grated chocolate and sifted confectioners' (icing) sugar can be sprinkled over the top, using strips of waxed (greaseproof) paper as a guide. Homemade truffles can also be rolled in finely grated chocolate to coat them.

Chocolate curls and shavings: use a thick bar of chocolate and make sure it is not too cold or too warm. Scrape a vegetable peeler along one long edge of the chocolate bar and let the curls fall onto a plate. Lift them carefully with a spatula onto the dessert or cake to be decorated.

Chocolate caraque: pour a thin layer of melted chocolate over a firm, flat surface, spreading quickly with a knife to make it smooth. Let stand until set then, holding the blade of a knife at a 45 degree angle, push it along the surface of the chocolate to form long scrolls. As the curls form, lift them carefully with the point of a knife. Chocolate caraque may be kept in a box in the refrigerator for a short while if necessary, until it is required.

Leaves: any fresh leaves may be used, as long as they are not poisonous. Rose leaves are particularly suitable because they have prominent veins and are an attractive shape. Wash and dry the leaves thoroughly, then brush the underside with melted chocolate. Alternatively, carefully dip the leaves into the melted chocolate. Place the leaves on waxed paper until completely set, then gently lift the tip of the leaf and peel it away from the chocolate.

Below: Chocolate curls, grated chocolate, and caraque for decoating cakes.

Piped chocolate: melted chocolate piped directly onto a cake or dessert is a very simple way of achieving a professional finish. It may be piped as writing or in a definite pattern, but even easier, and just as effective, is to drizzle the chocolate in a random pattern. Milk chocolate piped over semisweet, or the two combined in a piped design, look particularly attractive.

For piping chocolate, use a waxed paper bag with the end snipped off, or a pastry bag fitted with a fine writing tip. Alternatively, melt the chocolate in a plastic bag and pipe it straight from the bag (page 8). Keep your hand as cool as possible while piping, otherwise the chocolate will become too runny. If, however, the chocolate starts to set in the tip (nozzle) return it to a heatproof bowl set over a saucepan of hot water and it will soon soften.

Piped decorations: draw the outline of the required shape on nonstick paper as many times as needed. Melt the chocolate and pour into a waxed paper pastry bag. Let stand for a few seconds to cool and thicken slightly, then snip the end off the bag and pipe onto each drawn design. Carefully peel away from the paper when the chocolate is hard. Drawing an outline in melted semisweet chocolate, then filling in with milk chocolate when the outline has set can make attractive shapes or patterns. Let set until hard before removing each shape from the paper.

Below: *Selection of piped chocolate outlines from simple petals and hearts to butterflies and tortoise.*

Above: Cutting chocolate shapes. More complex shapes and therefore require a cookie or pastry cutter.

To make trellis cups: turn a muffin pan upside down and cover the pan with plastic wrap, pressing it down between the cups. Pipe a circle around the top and bottom edges of the cups, then pipe a trellis pattern all over each cup, making sure that all the lines join up. When set, carefully lift the trellis cups off the bun pan and peel away the plastic wrap.

Chocolate shapes: spread a thin layer of melted chocolate onto a sheet of nonstick paper. When just set, but not hard, cut out shapes with a cutter or knife. To cut squares, diamonds, rectangles, and triangles use a sharp knife that has been dipped in hot water and dried thoroughly. Cut the shape by pressing straight down without using a sawing motion. For more complex shapes use a metal cookie or pastry cutter, which has been dipped in hot water and dried thoroughly.

Very thin chocolate, such as cut out shapes, stale quickly and therefore should be used quickly. However, because these shapes are so thin and fragile it is advisable to keep them in the refrigerator. Providing they are left at room temperature to set and stored in the refrigerator in a covered box for as short a time as possible there is little risk of a "bloom" (page 7) developing.

Chocolate cups: pour cooled, melted chocolate into paper cake cases or petits four cases. Spread the chocolate evenly inside the cases with a brush or spoon, then let set. Once set, add another layer of chocolate, if desired. Let stand until set hard, then peel away the paper cases. Fill larger cups with fruit and cream or mousse mixtures, and smaller ones with nuts or truffle mixtures.

Shells: these make attractive containers for fruit, ice cream, and sherbet. Cover scallop shells with plastic wrap, then brush with an even layer of melted chocolate. Let stand until hard, then carefully peel away the plastic wrap.

Chocolate horns: cream horn pans can be used ideally as molds for chocolate horns. They are attractive as cake decorations, but they may also be used as edible cases for cream, fruit, ice cream, or truffle mixtures. Polish the inside of the cream horn pan with paper towels, dusted with a little cornstarch. Make sure that all traces of the cornstarch are removed before use. Pour in some melted chocolate, tilt the pan until evenly coated, then let stand until set. You can repeat the process to obtain a thicker layer of chocolate. Let stand until set hard, then carefully ease out of the pan.

– CHOCOLATE BAKED ALASKAS –

generous ¹/₃ cup (3 oz) butter or margarine
8 oz graham crackers
2 tablespoons semisweet chocolate chips
2¹/₂ cups chocolate ice cream
4 egg whites (see page 4)
pinch of salt
generous 1 cup superfine sugar
unsweetened cocoa, for dusting

Line a baking sheet with parchment paper. Melt butter. Place cookies and chocolate chips in a food processor and process. Stir in hot melted butter.

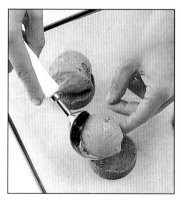

Continue processing until combined. Using a 2¹/₂-inch round cookie cutter as a template, press the mixture into 8 circles on the baking sheet. Freeze for 10 minutes. Dip an ice-cream scoop into hot water; scoop a ball of ice cream onto each cookie base. Return baking sheet to freezer for at least 1 hour.

Preheat oven to 425F (220C). Whisk egg whites and salt until very stiff. Add sugar, 1 tablespoon at a time, whisking after each spoonful. The mixture should be thick and glossy. Spoon or pipe a thick layer of meringue to cover the base and ice cream of each Alaska. Return to freezer for at least 4 hours or overnight. Bake 5–7 minutes, until golden. Serve at once dusted with cocoa.

Serves 8

── CHOCOLATE SOUFFLE ──

3 oz semisweet chocolate
²/³ cup milk
generous ¹/₄ cup superfine sugar
³/₈ cup all-purpose flour
1 tablespoon margarine
4 eggs, separated
1 tablespoon confectioners' sugar, sifted

Preheat oven to 400F (200C). Grease a 5-cup soufflé dish. In a small bowl set over a saucepan of simmering water, melt chocolate, stirring until smooth.

In a saucepan, heat milk and sugar gently until almost boiling. Add chocolate and mix well. In a bowl, blend flour with 2 tablespoons water. Gradually add chocolate mixture, blending well. Return to saucepan, bring gently to a boil, stirring constantly, and cook for 3 minutes. Add margarine in small pieces, mix well, then let cool.

Stir in egg yolks. In a bowl, whisk egg whites until stiff. Using a metal spoon, fold egg whites into chocolate mixture. Pour into soufflé dish and bake for 35 minutes, or until well risen and firm to the touch. Dust with sifted confectioners' sugar and serve immediately.

Serves 6

CLAFOUTIS AU CERISES

1 lb black cherries, pitted (or plums, pears, apples, red or black currants)
2 tablespoons granulated sugar
3 eggs
generous ¼ cup superfine sugar
³/8 cup self-rising flour
2 tablespoons unsweetened cocoa
²/3 cups heavy cream
1¼ cups milk
6 teaspoons kirsch
sifted confectioners' sugar, to decorate
CHOCOLATE CREAM:
1¼ cups heavy cream
4 oz semisweet chocolate, broken into pieces

Preheat oven to 375F (190C). Lightly grease a 9-inch ovenproof tart dish. Arrange cherries in dish, sprinkle with granulated sugar, and set aside. In a large bowl, whisk together the eggs and superfine sugar until light and frothy. Sift flour and cocoa onto a plate, add all at once to egg mixture, and beat in thoroughly. Whisk in cream, then milk and kirsch. Pour over cherries. Bake for 50–60 minutes, or until slightly risen and set in center.

Meanwhile, to make chocolate cream: in a saucepan, heat cream until almost boiling. Remove from heat, add chocolate, and stir until completely melted. Sift confectioners' sugar over clafoutis. Serve warm with chocolate cream.

Serves 6–8

— CHOCOLATE CREME BRULÉE —

7 oz semisweet chocolate, broken into pieces
3 cups heavy cream
6 large egg yolks
¹/₄ cup Grand Marnier or orange or almond liqueur
3 tablespoons light brown sugar

Preheat oven to 275F (140C). Place choco-late in a large heatproof bowl and set aside. In a saucepan, bring cream to a boil. Remove from heat and pour over chocolate. Let stand briefly, then stir until smooth.

In another bowl, whisk egg yolks and liqueur together. Add chocolate mixture. Stir until combined, then transfer to eight ²/₃-cup ramekins. Stand ramekins in a roasting pan just large enough to hold them all. Add boiling water to come halfway up sides of ramekins. Bake in center of oven 50 minutes, until just set. Let cool, then chill for about 4 hours, or until well chilled. Before serving, preheat broiler to its highest setting. Set the top shelf about 4–6 inches from element.

Sprinkle sugar evenly over surface of brulées and transfer to a baking sheet. Broil 3–4 minutes, or until sugar is bubbling and caramelized. Remove from broiler and let stand for 5 minutes, until sugar has set. Serve at once.

Makes 8

NOTE: do not broil too far ahead or the crisp topping will melt.

CHOCOLATE ZABAGLIONE

scant ¹/₂ cup superfine sugar
4 tablespoons rum
4 egg yolks
1 oz semisweet chocolate, finely grated
ladyfingers (see below), to serve

Place sugar, rum, and egg yolks in a bowl. Place over saucepan of gently simmering water and whisk until really thick and mousselike; this may take 5–7 minutes. Fold in the grated chocolate. Pour into 4 glasses and serve at once, with ladyfingers.

Ladyfingers: preheat oven to 375F (190C). In a large bowl set over a saucepan of hot water, whisk together 3 tablespoons superfine sugar and 1 egg until thick and mousselike. Carefully fold in 1 heaping tablespoon sifted all-purpose flour.

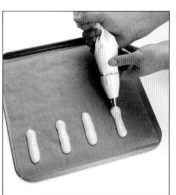

Using a pastry bag fitted with a ¹/₂-inch plain tip, pipe finger lengths of mixture onto a baking sheet lined with nonstick paper. Bake 6–8 minutes, until golden. Let cool on a wire rack.

Serves 4

LEMON BREAD PUDDING

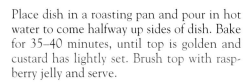

6–7 thin slices white bread, crusts removed
5 tablespoons butter, softened
1 cup fresh raspberries
7 oz good-quality white chocolate, broken into pieces
1 cup heavy cream
1 cup whole milk
1 lemon, zest only, removed in strips with potato
  peeler
3 eggs
3 tablespoons raspberry jelly, strained

Preheat oven to 375F (190C). Spread the slices of bread with butter and place a layer in the base of greased 6-cup shallow ovenproof dish.

Sprinkle over raspberries. Cut remaining bread into triangles and arrange on top. Place chocolate in heatproof bowl and set aside. In a saucepan, mix cream and milk together and add lemon zest. Bring to a boil. Pour mixture over the chocolate and let stand briefly. Whisk until smooth and let cool for 15 minutes. In another bowl, whisk eggs. Pour chocolate mixture over eggs and whisk together thoroughly. Pass through strainer, discarding lemon zest. Pour custard over bread and let soak for 5 minutes.

Place dish in a roasting pan and pour in hot water to come halfway up sides of dish. Bake for 35–40 minutes, until top is golden and custard has lightly set. Brush top with raspberry jelly and serve.

Serves 8

CHOCOLATE WAFFLES

4 tablespoons butter
2 oz semisweet chocolate, broken into pieces
generous 1 cup all-purpose flour
3 teaspoons baking powder
2 tablespoons superfine sugar
2 eggs, separated
1 1/4 cups milk
melted butter
TO SERVE:
butter, for spreading
honey, jelly, or maple syrup

In a small bowl set over a saucepan of simmering water, melt butter and chocolate, stirring until smooth. Let cool. Sift flour and baking powder into a large bowl. Stir in sugar. Make a well in center, drop in egg yolks, and mix thoroughly. Gradually add milk, alternating with chocolate and butter mixture. Beat thoroughly. In a bowl, whisk egg whites until stiff but not dry. Fold egg whites gently into chocolate batter.

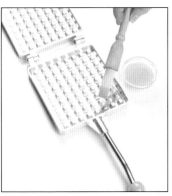

Brush a waffle iron with melted butter and heat until hot. Leave on medium hot. Pour in a little batter and close waffle iron, cook for about 1 minute on each side or until both sides of waffle are crisp and golden brown. Avoid piling waffles on top of each other or they will become soft very quickly. Serve with butter and honey, jelly, maple syrup, or whipped cream and cinnamon.

Makes about 10 depending on size and shape of waffle iron used.

— MOLTEN CHOCOLATE CAKES —

8 oz semisweet chocolate, broken into pieces
6 tablespoons butter
$\frac{1}{4}$ cup unsweetened cocoa
$\frac{1}{4}$ cup all-purpose flour
4 egg whites
4 tablespoons packed brown sugar
whipped cream, to serve

Preheat oven to 400F (200C). Grease and sugar eight muffin cups or ramekins. In top of a double boiler or in microwave, melt chocolate and butter, stirring frequently until smooth. Remove from heat, sift in cocoa and flour, and beat until smooth.

Meanwhile, in a clean bowl, beat egg whites until soft peaks form. Add sugar and beat until stiff and glossy. Fold one-third of egg white mixture into chocolate mixture with a metal spoon until incorporated. Gently fold in rest.

Fill cups or ramekins about two thirds full. You may prepare cakes up to this point and chill for several days. Bake 5–7 minutes, until risen and cracked on top, but still runny in center. Let cakes stand for a few minutes, turn out, and serve at once with whipped cream.

Makes 8

NOTE: The cakes will take 2–3 minutes longer if you cook them straight from the refrigerator.

──── CHOCOLATE PECAN PIE ────

PIE DOUGH:
1 cup all-purpose flour
pinch of salt
1/3 cup (3 oz) butter
FILLING:
3/4 cup superfine sugar
1 1/4 cups corn syrup
2 oz semisweet chocolate, coarsely chopped
1/4 cup (2 oz) butter
4 extra large eggs, lightly beaten
2 cups pecan halves
whipped cream, to serve

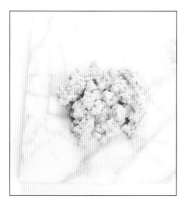

Place flour and salt in a food processor, add butter, and pulse until mixture is crumbly. Add 4 tablespoons water and pulse again until mixture starts to form a ball. Knead dough into a ball. Chill 30 minutes. Preheat oven to 400F (200C). Roll dough out thinly and line a 9-inch fluted tart pan. Prick base with a fork, but do not puncture dough. Line with waxed paper and fill with ceramic beans. Bake 12 minutes, then remove paper and beans. Bake a further 5 minutes, until dry. Remove from oven, reducing temperature to 350F (180C).

In a saucepan, slowly bring sugar and syrup to a boil over medium-low heat, stirring constantly. Remove from heat, add chocolate and butter, stir until smooth. Add a little chocolate mixture to eggs and quickly stir in. Add egg mixture to remaining chocolate mixture. Whisk until just blended. Add pecans, stir, then pour into pie shell. Bake in center of oven 45–50 minutes, until filling appears set, but slightly wobbly in center. Let cool on wire rack.

Serves 8–10

MINTY MOUSSE

6 oz semisweet chocolate
1¼ cups heavy cream
1 egg (see page 4)
pinch of salt
few drops peppermint extract
½ recipe Chocolate Cups (page 22, optional)
coarsely grated semisweet chocolate, to decorate
   (optional)
SUGARED MINT LEAVES:
fresh mint leaves
1 small egg white (see page 4)
superfine sugar

Break up chocolate in small pieces and place in a blender or food processor fitted with a metal blade. In a small saucepan, heat heavy cream until almost boiling. Pour cream over chocolate and process for 1 minute. Add egg, salt, and peppermint extract and process for an additional 1 minute. Pour into individual ramekins or chocolate cups, if desired and let chill overnight.

To prepare decoration: wash and dry mint leaves. In a shallow bowl, lightly whisk egg white and dip in mint leaves to cover. Dip leaves into sugar, shake off any excess, and let stand on waxed paper until hardened. To serve, decorate mousses with sugared mint leaves and grated chocolate, if desired.

Serves 4–6

NOTE: Peppermint extract has a very strong flavor; use it sparingly.

— CHOCOLATE MOUSSE CUPS —

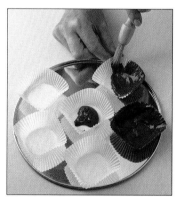

5 oz white chocolate, broken into pieces
grated rind and juice of 1 orange
$^{1}/_{4}$ oz ($1^{1}/_{2}$ teaspoons) envelope unflavored gelatin
2 eggs, separated (see page 4)
$^{3}/_{4}$ cup heavy cream
$^{1}/_{2}$ cup dairy sour cream
CHOCOLATE CUPS:
12 oz semisweet chocolate, broken into pieces
3 tablespoons butter
TO DECORATE (Optional):
shredded orange rind
tiny edible flowers

To prepare chocolate cups: melt semisweet chocolate, stirring until smooth. Stir in butter. Using a pastry brush, brush chocolate over base and sides of 12 paper cups. Chill until hardened. Meanwhile, to prepare mousse: melt white chocolate with half of orange juice, stirring until smooth. In a small bowl, sprinkle gelatin over remaining orange juice and let stand 2–3 minutes, until softened. Set bowl over a saucepan of hot water and stir until gelatin has dissolved. Stir into chocolate mixture with orange rind. Let cool.

Beat egg yolks into cooled chocolate mixture. In a bowl, whip cream and sour cream. In a separate bowl, whisk egg whites until stiff. Fold whipped creams, then egg whites into chocolate mixture and let chill until almost set. Spoon mousse into chocolate cups and let chill until mousse has set. Peel away paper cups before serving. Decorate with orange rind and flowers, if desired.

Makes 12

MOCHA WHIP

2 oz semisweet chocolate, broken into pieces
$^1/_2$ teaspoon instant coffee granules
3 teaspoons granulated gelatin
1$^1/_4$ cups very lowfat fromage frais
1$^1/_4$ cups lowfat fromage frais
6 teaspoons thin honey
4 oz trifle sponge cakes, broken coarsely into pieces
TO DECORATE:
fresh fruit
chocolate vermicelli

In a bowl set over a saucepan of simmering water, melt chocolate, stirring until smooth. Let cool.

Dissolve coffee granules in 1 tablespoon warm water. In a small bowl, sprinkle gelatin over 3 tablespoons water and let stand 2–3 minutes to soften. Set bowl over a saucepan of hot water and stir until gelatin has dissolved. Let cool. In a separate bowl, mix together chocolate, coffee, gelatin, fromage frais, and honey until thoroughly combined. If, at this stage, mixture starts to harden, set bowl over a saucepan of hot water for a few minutes until mixture softens again.

Layer mocha mixture and trifle sponge cakes in individual glass dishes or one large glass serving dish, finishing with a mocha layer. Let chill until set. Decorate with fresh fruit and chocolate vermicelli and serve.

Serves 6

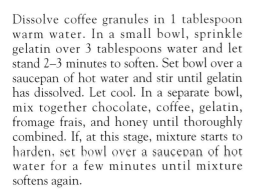

— PETIT POTS AU CHOCOLAT —

2¹/₂ cups light cream or milk
1 vanilla bean
1 egg
5 egg yolks
3 tablespoons superfine sugar
8 oz semisweet chocolate, chopped
1 tablespoon instant coffee granules
TO DECORATE:
whipped cream
chocolate shavings

Place cream and vanilla bean in a saucepan and bring to a boil over low heat. Cover, remove from heat, and let infuse for 15 minutes.

Preheat oven to 300F (150C). Grease individual ramekins and place in a roasting pan. Place egg, egg yolks, and sugar in a large bowl and whisk together until thick and pale. Remove vanilla bean from cream and return to a boil.

Remove from heat, add chocolate, and coffee and stir until dissolved. Stir into egg mixture. Strain into ramekins. Pour boiling water into roasting pan to come halfway up sides of ramekins and bake for 1 hour, or until very lightly set. Transfer ramekins to a wire rack and let cool, and then chill. Decorate with whipped cream and chocolate shavings and serve.

Serves 6–8

ST EMILION DESSERT

6 oz amaretti cookies or almond macaroons
1 tablespoon brandy
1 tablespoon almond liqueur
$^1\!/_2$ cup (4 oz) unsalted butter
$^1\!/_2$ cup superfine sugar
8 oz semisweet chocolate, melted (page 7)
1$^1\!/_4$ cups milk
2 eggs, beaten
TO DECORATE:
3 tablespoons heavy cream
chocolate leaves (page 9)

Arrange a layer of amaretti cookies at the bottom of a glass bowl.

In a small bowl, mix together brandy and almond liqueur. Sprinkle cookies with half the brandy mixture. Place remaining cookies on a plate and sprinkle with remaining brandy mixture. In a bowl, cream together butter and sugar until light and fluffy. Stir in melted chocolate. In a saucepan, heat milk until almost boiling; stir into beaten eggs and return to pan. Stir over low heat until mixture thickens and coats the back of the spoon. Stir slowly into chocolate mixture. Let chill until just starting to set.

Spoon half the chocolate mixture over amaretti cookies in dish. Arrange soaked cookies on top. Cover with remaining chocolate mixture. Let chill for several hours or overnight.

To serve: whip cream and decorate top of dessert with cream and chocolate leaves.

Serves 6–8

NOTE: This dessert looks most attractive in individual glass dishes.

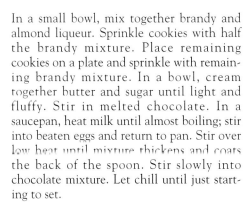

CHOCOLATE PEARS

2 oz amaretti cookies (macaroons)
3–4 tablespoons Cointreau
4 oz semisweet chocolate, broken into pieces
3 tablespoons strong coffee
1 tablespoon orange juice
2 tablespoons butter
2 eggs, separated (see page 4)
4 ripe medium-size pears
TO DECORATE (Optional):
orange rind curls
fresh mint sprigs

Place amaretti cookies in a bowl. Pour liqueur over cookies. Using end of a rolling pin, crush cookies to rough crumbs.

In top of double boiler or bowl set over a saucepan of simmering water, melt chocolate with coffee and orange juice, stirring until smooth. Remove from heat and beat in butter and egg yolks. In a separate bowl, whisk egg whites until stiff, then fold chocolate mixture into them. Set aside. Peel pears, leaving them whole with stems intact. Hollow out as much core as possible from bottom and fill cavity with crumb mixture.

Set pears on a wire rack, cutting off a small slice to make them stand upright, if necessary. Spoon chocolate mixture over pears to coat evenly. Let chill for several hours or overnight. To serve, place on serving plates and decorate with orange rind and mint, if desired.

Serves 4

CHOCOLATE TRIFLE

3¹/₂ oz semisweet chocolate, broken into pieces
2 tablespoons rum
2 tablespoons water
4 egg yolks (see page 4)
1 tablespoon superfine sugar
3 cups heavy cream
8 oz plain or trifle sponge cakes
¹/₂ cup apricot jelly
12 oz mixed fruit, such as grapes, ripe pears, and
   bananas
grated semisweet chocolate to decorate (optional)

In a bowl set over a saucepan of simmering
water, melt chocolate with rum and water,
stirring until smooth.

In a large bowl, whisk egg yolks and sugar
until light and fluffy. In a saucepan, bring
whipping cream almost to boiling point.
Whisk into egg yolk mixture with melted
chocolate mixture. Return mixture to
saucepan and whisk over very low heat until
chocolate is incorporated and mixture has
thickened slightly. Slice sponge cakes in
half. In a small saucepan, warm jelly slightly
and brush over sponge cakes.

Place sponge cakes in serving dishes. Halve
and seed grapes, peel, core, and finely slice
pears, and slice bananas. Sprinkle fruit over
sponge cakes. Lightly whip remaining
cream. Spoon chocolate sauce over fruit and
spread whipped cream over chocolate sauce.
Decorate with grated chocolate, if desired.
Let chill until ready to serve.

Serves 6

— CHOCOLATE PROFITEROLES —

CHOUX PASTRY:
¹/₄ cup (2 oz) butter, cubed
scant ¹/₂ cup all-purpose flour, sifted
2 eggs, beaten
TO SERVE:
1¹/₄ cups heavy cream
hot Dark Chocolate Sauce (page 87)

Preheat oven to 400F (200C). Line 2 baking sheets with parchment paper. Place butter and ²/₃ cup water in a saucepan, set over medium heat. When butter has melted, bring to a boil, then remove from heat. Add flour and beat until mixture leaves sides of saucepan.

Gradually beat eggs into flour mixture until dough is smooth and shiny. Place dough in a pastry bag and pipe walnut-size mounds onto baking sheets. Bake 20–25 minutes, until brown, puffed up, and just crisp on the outside. Make a small hole in side of each profiterole. This allows steam to escape and helps keep them crisp.

Cool profiteroles on a wire rack. When ready to serve, whip cream stiffly. Enlarge hole in side of each profiterole and pipe cream into them. Serve profiteroles with hot sauce poured over them.

Serves 4

NOTE: for speed and ease, you can use a food processor to beat the eggs into the flour mixture.

– CHOCOLATE BRANDY CREAMS –

3 oz semisweet chocolate, broken into pieces
²/₃ cup light cream
1¹/₄ cups heavy cream
1 tablespoon confectioners' sugar, sifted
2 tablespoons brandy
chocolate curls (page 9), to decorate
almond curls (see below), to serve

Place chocolate and light cream in a saucepan and heat very gently until chocolate has melted. Stir mixture until smooth and let cool.

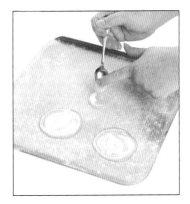

In a bowl, whip heavy cream until thick, then carefully whisk in sugar, brandy, and chocolate mixture, taking care not to over-whip. Spoon into 6 tall glasses and sprinkle with chocolate curls. Let chill until required. Serve with Almond Curls.

Almond curls: preheat oven to 400F (200C). In a bowl, mix ¹/₄ cup sifted all-purpose flour with ¹/₄ cup superfine sugar. Make a well in center and add 1 egg white and 2 tablespoons melted butter. Mix until smooth. Place teaspoonfuls of mixture onto greased and floured baking sheets. Spread into 2¹/₂-inch circles and sprinkle with ¹/₈ cup slivered almonds. Bake 6–7 minutes, until pale golden. Using a palette knife, curl over a rolling pin. Let stand until firm.

Serves 6

FEATHER-LIGHT TIRAMISU

3 tablespoons very strong cold espresso coffee
1 tablespoon brandy or rum
few drops of vanilla extract
1/2 cup vanilla sugar
1 cup reduced-fat cream cheese
1/2 cup reduced-fat sour cream
2 egg whites (see page 4)
18 ladyfingers
2 oz bittersweet chocolate, grated

In a bowl, mix together coffee, vanilla, and brandy. In another bowl, beat sugar and cream cheese together.

Whisk sour cream until just holding its shape and fold into cream cheese mixture. In a clean bowl, whisk egg whites until forming stiff peaks, then fold into cheese and cream mixture.

Break half the ladyfingers into pieces and place on base of 6 glasses. Drizzle with half the coffee mixture. Spoon on half the cream mixture and sprinkle with half the grated chocolate. Repeat with the remaining ingredients, finishing with grated chocolate. Let chill until firm and serve within 1 day.

Serves 6

CHOCOLATE ROULADE

ROULADE:
4 eggs, separated
$^1/_2$ cup superfine sugar
4 oz semisweet chocolate, melted (page 7)
FILLING:
1 cup heavy cream
5 oz white chocolate
sifted confectioners' sugar, for sprinkling
chocolate leaves (page 7), to decorate

Preheat oven to 350F (180C). Line a 9 x 13-inch jelly roll pan with nonstick paper.

To make roulade: in a bowl, whisk together egg yolks and sugar until thick and pale. Gently fold in cooled melted chocolate. In another bowl, whisk egg whites until stiff. Carefully fold into chocolate mixture. Pour into pan and bake 20–25 minutes, until firm. Cover with a dishtowel and leave in pan overnight. To make filling: in a saucepan, heat cream to just below boiling point. In a food processor, chop white chocolate. With motor still running, pour hot cream through feed tube. Process for 10–15 seconds, until mixture is smooth.

Transfer mixture to a bowl, cover with plastic wrap, and chill overnight. Whisk filling until it starts to form soft peaks. Sprinkle a sheet of waxed paper with sifted confectioners' sugar. Turn roulade onto paper. Peel away lining paper. Spread filling over roulade and roll up, starting at a short side. Transfer to serving dish. Let chill for 2–3 hours. Decorate with chocolate leaves before serving.

Serves 6–8

— TWO CHOCOLATE TERRINE —

WHITE CHOCOLATE MOUSSE:
9 oz white chocolate
1½ teaspoons granulated gelatin
1 heaping tablespoon liquid glucose
2 egg yolks (see page 4)
⅔ cup heavy cream
⅔ cup thick sour cream
DARK CHOCOLATE MOUSSE:
6 oz semisweet chocolate
4 tablespoons strong black coffee
2 teaspoons granulated gelatine
½ cup (4 oz) butter, cut into cubes
2 egg yolks (see page 4)
1¼ cups heavy cream

Line a 2¼-lb loaf pan with plastic wrap to overlap edges. To make white chocolate mousse: break white chocolate into small pieces and set aside. In a small bowl, sprinkle gelatin over 2 tablespoons water and let soften 2–3 minutes. In a saucepan, place 3 tablespoons water and glucose and bring to a boil. Remove from heat and stir in gelatin until dissolved. Add chocolate and beat mixture until chocolate has melted and is smooth.

Beat in egg yolks, one at a time. In a bowl, whip creams together lightly and fold into chocolate mixture. Pour chocolate into loaf pan. Let chill until set.

To make dark chocolate mousse: in top of double boiler or bowl set over a saucepan of simmering water, melt chocolate with coffee stirring until smooth. In a small bowl, sprinkle gelatin over 3 tablespoons water and let soften 2–3 minutes. Set bowl over a saucepan of hot water and stir until gelatin has dissolved. Stir into chocolate with butter and beat until butter has melted and everything is mixed. Let cool, then beat in egg yolks. In a bowl, whip cream lightly and fold into chocolate mixture.

Pour dark chocolate mixture over set white chocolate mousse in pan. Let chill until set, then cover with overlapping plastic wrap and let chill overnight.

When ready to serve, unfold plastic wrap from top of mousse and turn out onto a serving dish. Carefully peel off plastic wrap and decorate terrine with whipped cream and grated chocolate. Serve cut into slices.

Serves 8–10

NOTE: serve with Dark Chocolate Sauce (page 87), if desired. Either mousse can be served as a dessert on its own and will serve 4 people.

CAROB-HAZELNUT CHEESECAKE

²/₃ cup whole-wheat all-purpose flour
generous ¹/₈ cup carob flour
¹/₄ cup (2 oz) lowfat spread
³/₅ cup semisweet carob chips
1 cup lowfat soft cheese
²/₃ cup very lowfat fromage frais
12 teaspoons thick honey
scant ¹/₄ cup hazelnuts, chopped
2 eggs, separated
1 tablespoon confectioners' sugar, sifted

Preheat oven to 350F (180C). Sift both flours into a bowl. Rub in lowfat spread until mixture resembles bread crumbs. Add enough water to make a soft dough.

On a lightly floured surface, roll out dough and use to line base of an 8-inch loose-bottom tart pan. In a small bowl set over a saucepan of simmering water, melt carob chips. Let cool. In a large bowl, mix together melted carob, soft cheese, fromage frais, honey, nuts, and egg yolks until well combined. In another bowl, whisk egg whites until stiff and fold gently into carob mixture, using a metal spoon.

Pour mixture over dough base. Bake 45 minutes, until firm to the touch. Let cool on a wire rack, then let chill. To serve, remove cheesecake from pan and dust with sifted confectioners' sugar.

Serves 8

NOTE: Serve with yogurt and chopped nuts, if desired.

- MOLDED CHOCOLATE PUDDING -

9 oz semisweet chocolate, broken into pieces
1/4 cup plus 1 tablespoon strong coffee
3/4 cup (6 oz) unsalted butter, diced
3/4 cup superfine sugar
4 large eggs, beaten
1 1/2 cups heavy cream
tiny edible flowers, to decorate (optional)

Preheat oven to 350F (175C). Line a 4-cup bowl or soufflé dish with double thickness of foil.

In top of double boiler or bowl set over a saucepan of simmering water, melt chocolate with coffee. Gradually beat in butter and sugar and heat until mixture is hot and butter melts. Remove from heat and gradually whisk in eggs. Strain mixture into dish, cover with foil, and place in a roasting pan. Add enough boiling water to pan to come halfway up dish. Bake 1 hour, until top has thick crust. Let cool, then let chill.

To serve: unmold pudding onto a serving dish and carefully peel away foil. In a bowl, whip cream until stiff, then cover pudding with two-third whipped cream. Using a pastry bag fitted with a star tip, pipe remaining cream in rosettes around top and bottom of pudding. Decorate with edible flowers, if desired.

Serves 6–8

—— CHOCOLATE CHEESECAKE ——

BASE:
5 oz semisweet chocolate cookies
1/4 cup (2 oz) butter
1/4 teaspoon ground cinnamon
FILLING:
11 lb cream cheese
3/4 cup superfine sugar
2 eggs
1 dessertspoon unsweetened cocoa
1 teaspoon vanilla extract
1 1/4 cups sour cream
5 oz semisweet chocolate, melted (page 7)
grated chocolate, to decorate

Preheat oven to 212F (100C). For base: crush cookies until crumbled. Melt butter and add cookie crumbs and cinnamon. Mix together and turn into a 9-inch tart pan. Let chill until set. Beat cream cheese and superfine sugar together. When light and fluffy, add eggs one at a time and beat thoroughly. Add cocoa, vanilla extract, and sour cream and beat well; the mixture will be quite runny. Add melted chocolate and mix well.

Turn onto chilled cookie base and bake for 1 hour 10 minutes. The edges of cheesecake should be firm but center may still be slightly soft. Remove from oven, let cool, then let chill for 4 hours or overnight if you want to prepare in advance. Decorate with grated chocolate and serve.

Serves 6–8

ZUCOTTO

scant ²/₃ cup (3¹/₂ oz) self-rising flour
2 tablespoons unsweetened cocoa
¹/₂ teaspoon baking powder
generous ¹/₂ cup (4 oz) superfine sugar
¹/₂ cup (4 oz) soft margarine
2 eggs
3 tablespoons brandy
3 tablespoons cherry brandy
FILLING:
1¹/₄ cups (10 fl oz) heavy cream
¹/₄ cup (1 oz) confectioners' sugar
¹/₂ cup (3 oz) chopped hazelnuts, toasted
1¹/₂ cups (10 oz) black cherries, pitted
2 oz semisweet chocolate, grated or finely chopped
TO DECORATE:
3 teaspoons unsweetened cocoa
3 teaspoons confectioners' sugar

Preheat oven to 375F (190C). Grease and line a 12 x 9-inch jelly roll pan. Sift flour, cocoa, and baking powder into a bowl. Add sugar, margarine, and eggs. Beat thoroughly until well mixed. Pour into pan and bake 15–20 minutes, or until well risen and firm to the touch. Turn onto a wire rack to cool. Using rim of a 5-cup (2-pint) ovenproof bowl as a guide cut a circle from cake. Line bowl with plastic wrap, then with remaining cake, cutting as necessary to fit.

In a bowl, mix together brandy and cherry brandy. Sprinkle over sponge, including cutout circle. To make filling: in a bowl, whip cream and confectioners' sugar together until stiff. Fold in hazelnuts, cherries, and chocolate. Fill sponge mold with cream mixture. Press sponge circle on top. Cover with a plate and weight. Let chill for several hours or overnight. Turn out onto a serving plate. Decorate with cocoa and confectioners' sugar, in alternating segments.

Serves 6

STRAWBERRY ROULADE

3 eggs
generous ¹/₂ cup superfine sugar
generous ¹/₂ cup all-purpose flour
generous ¹/₄ cup unsweetened cocoa
1 cup skim milk soft cheese
12 teaspoons strawberry jelly
generous 1 cup strawberries
1 tablespoon confectioners' sugar, sifted

Preheat oven to 400F (200C). Grease a 13 x 9-inch jelly roll pan. Line with waxed paper and grease paper. In a bowl placed over a saucepan of hot water, whisk eggs and sugar until creamy.

Remove bowl from heat and whisk until cool. Sift flour and cocoa over egg mixture, add 1 tablespoon hot water, and fold in gently with a metal spoon. Pour mixture into pan and tilt to level surface. Bake 12–15 minutes, until well risen, golden brown, and firm to the touch. Turn out onto a sheet of waxed paper, cut off crisp edges, and roll up with paper inside. Let cool.

Unroll gently and spread with soft cheese and jelly. Slice strawberries and place on jelly, reserving a few for decoration. Roll up again and place on a serving dish. Dust with sifted confectioners' sugar and decorate with remaining strawberry slices before serving.

Serves 6

CHOCOLATE ALMOND MERINGUE

MERINGUE:
4 egg whites
generous 1 cup superfine sugar
generous 1 cup ground almonds
FILLING:
6 oz semisweet chocolate, broken into pieces
3 tablespoons unsalted butter
3 tablespoons black coffee
3 tablespoons brandy
3/4 cup heavy cream
toasted almonds, chopped, to decorate

Preheat oven to 275F (140C). Line 2 baking sheets with nonstick paper.

To make meringue: mix egg whites in a bowl until stiff; whisk in half the sugar. In another bowl, mix together remaining sugar and ground almonds. Carefully fold into meringue mixture. Pipe or spread meringue in two 8-inch circles on prepared baking sheets. Bake for 1¹/₂ hours, or until completely dry. Let cool on wire racks.

To make filling: place chocolate in a bowl with butter, coffee, and brandy. Set over a saucepan of simmering water. When melted, stir, and let cool. Whip cream lightly. Stir in chocolate mixture. Sandwich meringue circles together with most of chocolate cream. Place remaining cream into a pastry bag and pipe rosettes on top of cake. Decorate with toasted almonds.

Serves 8

– CHOCOLATE CHESTNUT TART –

8 oz gingersnap cookies, crushed
6 tablespoons butter, melted
FILLING:
6 oz unsweetened chestnut purée
1/4 cup superfine sugar
few drops vanilla extract
3/4 cup ricotta cheese
2 eggs
3 1/2 oz semisweet chocolate, melted (page 7)
generous 1/4 cup ground almonds
TO DECORATE:
2/3 cup heavy cream, whipped
grated chocolate
chocolate diamond shapes (page 11)

Preheat oven to 350F (180C). Combine cookie crumbs and melted butter. Press onto base and up sides of a 9-inch loose-bottom tart pan. Bake for 10 minutes, then let cool. To make filling: in a bowl, beat together chestnut purée, sugar, and vanilla extract until smooth. In another bowl, beat together ricotta cheese and eggs until smooth. Stir melted chocolate into cheese mixture. Add chestnut mixture and mix well. Stir in almonds. Pour filling into tart pan and bake for 35 minutes, or until lightly set. Let cool, then chill thoroughly.

Before serving, spread a thin layer of cream over the top and sprinkle with grated chocolate. Pipe remaining cream around edge and decorate with chocolate diamonds.

Serves 6–8

NOTE: if unsweetened chestnut purée is unavailable, the sweetened version may be used. Omit sugar and vanilla from recipe, as sweetened chestnut purée usually tastes quite strongly of vanilla, and expect a sweeter result.

— CHOCOLATE CHERRY SLICE —

6 oz semisweet chocolate, broken into pieces
4 eggs
generous ¼ cup superfine sugar
generous ¼ cup all-purpose flour
FILLING:
7¼ oz canned unsweetened chestnut purée
4 oz semisweet chocolate, melted (page 7)
1¼ cups heavy cream
9 teaspoons morello cherry jelly
1 cup fresh or canned cherries, pitted and halved

Preheat oven to 375F (190C). Line a 13 x 9-inch jelly roll pan with nonstick paper. In a bowl set over a saucepan of simmering water, melt chocolate, stirring until smooth.

Whisk eggs and sugar until pale and thick enough to leave a trail. Stir in chocolate, sift in flour, and fold in gently. Transfer to pan, shake to level, and bake 20–25 minutes, until firm to the touch. Cover with a damp dishtowel; let stand until cold. To make filling: place chestnut purée and chocolate in a food processor fitted with a metal blade. Process until puréed. Fold in two-thirds cream. Stiffly whip remaining cream. Place in a pastry bag fitted with a small star tip.

Turn cake out of pan and remove paper. Trim edges and cut into 3 short strips across width. Spread 2 strips of cake with jelly, then cover with one-third chestnut mixture. Arrange one-third cherry halves on each. Stack layers together on a serving plate with remaining cake layer on top. Spread top and sides with remaining chestnut mixture and pipe cream around top edge. Decorate with remaining cherry halves. Let chill.

Serves 10

— CHOCOLATE TRUFFLE TART —

PIE DOUGH:
1 cup all-purpose flour
pinch of salt
¹/₄ cup superfine sugar
¹/₃ cup (3 oz) butter, cut into small cubes
FILLING:
1 cup heavy cream
8 oz semisweet chocolate, broken into pieces
2 eggs, lightly beaten
TO DECORATE:
confectioners' sugar
unsweetened cocoa

To make dough: refer to instructions for Chocolate Pecan Pie (page 20), but bake pastry shell an additional 10 minutes once paper and beans have been removed, until dry and lightly golden. Meanwhile, for the filling: in a medium saucepan, bring cream to a boil. Remove from heat and add chocolate. Let stand for 1 minute. Stir until completely smooth. Let mixture cool to room temperature.

Whisk in eggs until just incorporated. Pour into pastry shell and bake 12–15 minutes. The center will wobble when lightly shaken. Let cool on wire rack before serving in small wedges, decorated with confectioners' sugar and cocoa.

Serves 12

— CHOCOLATE MARBLE CAKE —

2 oz semisweet chocolate, broken into pieces
3 teaspoons strong coffee
1½ cups self-rising flour
1 teaspoon baking powder
1 cup (8 oz) soft margarine
generous 1 cup superfine sugar
4 eggs, beaten
½ cup ground almonds
6 teaspoons milk
FROSTING:
4½ oz semisweet chocolate, broken into pieces
2 tablespoons butter

Preheat oven to 350F (180C). Grease a 7½-cup ring mold. In a bowl set over a saucepan of simmering water, heat chocolate and coffee, stirring constantly, until melted and smooth. Let cool. Sift flour and baking powder into a bowl. Add margarine, sugar, eggs, ground almonds, and milk. Beat well until smooth. Spoon half the mixture evenly into mold. Stir cooled, soft chocolate into remaining mixture, and spoon into mold. Draw a knife through mixture in a spiral. Smooth the surface.

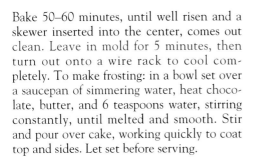

Bake 50–60 minutes, until well risen and a skewer inserted into the center, comes out clean. Leave in mold for 5 minutes, then turn out onto a wire rack to cool completely. To make frosting: in a bowl set over a saucepan of simmering water, heat chocolate, butter, and 6 teaspoons water, stirring constantly, until melted and smooth. Stir and pour over cake, working quickly to coat top and sides. Let set before serving.

Serves 10–12

RICH CHOCOLATE LOG

14 oz canned sweetened condensed milk
3 oz semisweet chocolate, broken into pieces
3 tablespoons butter
1 lb plain sponge cake
²/₃ cup candied cherries, halved
¹/₂ cup walnuts, chopped
3 tablespoons chopped pitted dates
CHOCOLATE FUDGE FROSTING:
3 tablespoons butter
¹/₄ cup superfine sugar
¹/₂ cup confectioners' sugar
¹/₄ cup unsweetened cocoa
TO DECORATE (Optional):
candied cherries, cut into strips
walnut halves

In a saucepan, combine milk, chocolate, and butter. Stir over low heat until chocolate and butter have melted and ingredients are well combined. Remove from heat. In a blender or food processor fitted with the metal blade, process cake to crumbs. Stir crumbs into chocolate mixture. Stir in cherries, walnuts, and dates. Spoon mixture onto a large piece of waxed paper and form into log shape. Roll up in waxed paper. Chill overnight.

Two hours before serving, unwrap log and place on a serving dish. To prepare frosting: in a saucepan, combine butter, superfine sugar, and water. Bring to a boil. Sift confectioners' sugar and cocoa into saucepan and beat well. Cool until fudgy, then spread over roll. Mark lines along roll with fork. Decorate with candied cherry strips and walnut halves, if desired.

Serves 8–10

— CHOCOLATE MINI MUFFINS —

scant 1 cup self-rising flour
2 1/2 tablespoons unsweetened cocoa
1 teaspoon baking powder
pinch of salt
generous 1/4 cup soft packed brown sugar
1 small egg, lightly beaten
2/3 cup milk
1/4 cup (2 oz) butter, melted and cooled slightly
1/2 teaspoon vanilla extract
chocolate and hazelnut spread or chocolate frosting,
  for filling

Preheat oven to 400F (200C). Grease 20 mini muffin cups, about 1 3/4 x 1/4 inches, or place small paper cases in cups. Sift flour, cocoa, baking powder, and salt into a shallow bowl. Stir in sugar. Stir egg into milk, butter, and vanilla extract. Pour onto dry ingredients and mix briefly using a large metal spoon and a lifting figure-of-eight movement; there should not be any free flour but batter should still be lumpy.

One-third to half-fill paper cases or muffin pans with batter. Place 1/2–1 teaspoon of spread or frosting on each portion of batter and cover with more batter so that cases or cups are almost filled. Bake 20 minutes, until risen and tops spring back when lightly touched. Paper cases can be removed immediately. Alternatively place cups on a wire rack and let cool 5 minutes, then remove muffins from cups. Serve warm.

Makes about 20

— CHOCOLATE NUT MUFFINS —

1 cup walnuts
4 oz semisweet chocolate, broken into pieces
1¹/2 cups all-purpose flour
3 teaspoons baking powder
¹/2 teaspoon ground cinnamon
generous ¹/4 cup soft packed brown sugar
1 cup milk
¹/4 cup corn or sunflower oil
few drops vanilla extract
1 egg

Preheat oven to 400F (200C). Grease a 12-hole muffin or deep bun pan. Coarsely chop walnuts. Set aside.

In a bowl set over a saucepan of simmering water, melt chocolate, stirring constantly, until smooth. Remove from heat.

Sift flour, baking powder, and cinnamon into chocolate. Add sugar and nuts. In a bowl, mix together milk, oil, vanilla extract, and egg; add to dry ingredients and stir until blended. Spoon mixture into pan. Bake 15–20 minutes, until well risen and firm. Let cool in pan 5 minutes. Remove to a wire rack to cool completely.

Makes 12

GATEAU GRENOBLE

¹/₃ cup hazelnuts, skinned
4 eggs, separated, plus 1 egg white
¹/₂ cup plus 1 tablespoon superfine sugar
3 oz semisweet chocolate, broken into pieces
2¹/₂ cups walnuts, finely chopped, plus extra to
  decorate (optional)
fresh mint leaves, to decorate (optional)
whipped cream, to serve

Preheat oven to 300F (150C). Generously grease an 8 x 4-inch loaf pan. Grind hazelnuts in coffee grinder. In a large bowl, beat egg yolks, then gradually beat in ¹/₂ cup of sugar, until mixture is light and fluffy.

In top of a double boiler or a bowl set over a saucepan of simmering water, melt chocolate and stir into yolk mixture with hazelnuts and walnuts. In a large bowl, whisk egg whites until stiff but not dry. Sprinkle in remaining sugar and whisk again until mixture is glossy; fold 2–3 tablespoons into chocolate mixture.

Carefully fold remaining egg white into chocolate mixture. (This is quite hard to do as mixture is very stiff; keep cutting and folding until incorporated.) Pour into prepared pan and place in a roasting pan. Add boiling water to come halfway up pan. Cover and bake for 1¹/₂ hours; let cool. Slice and serve with whipped cream. Sprinkle with extra chopped walnuts on whipped cream and decorate with mint leaves, if desired.

Serves 6

– DOUBLE CHOCOLATE GATEAU –

generous 1 cup each soft butter,
  superfine sugar, self-rising flour
4 eggs, beaten
generous ¹/₂ cup unsweetened cocoa
FILLING:
1 cup heavy cream
5 oz white chocolate
FROSTING:
12 oz semisweet chocolate, broken into pieces
¹/₂ cup (4 oz) butter
¹/₃ cup heavy cream
TO DECORATE:
chocolate shavings (page 9)
4 oz semisweet chocolate, broken into pieces
2 teaspoons confectioners' sugar and unsweetened
  cocoa mixed

To make filling: heat cream to just below boiling point. In a food processor, chop white chocolate. Keep motor running, pour hot cream through feed tube and process 10–15 seconds, until smooth. Transfer to a bowl, cover with plastic wrap, and chill overnight. Whisk the filling until just starting to hold soft peaks.

To make chocolate curls for decoration: in a bowl set over a saucepan of hot water, melt chocolate, stirring constantly until smooth. Spread one-quarter of chocolate over a baking sheet. Chill sheet for a few minutes until chocolate loses its gloss and is just set, but not hard. Using a palette knife, scrape off large shavings of chocolate, transferring them to a baking sheet lined with nonstick paper. Chill until set. Make 3 more batches of shavings in the same way.

Serves 10

Preheat oven to 350F (180C). Grease an 8-inch deep round cake pan and line base with nonstick paper. In a bowl, beat butter and sugar together until light and fluffy. Gradually beat in eggs. Sift together flour and cocoa. Fold into batter, then spoon into pan. Bake 45–50 minutes, until springy to touch and a skewer inserted into center comes out clean. Leave in pan 5 minutes, then let cool completely on wire rack.

To make frosting: in a bowl set over a saucepan of simmering water, melt chocolate. Stir in butter and cream. Let cool, stirring occasionally, until a thick spreading consistency.

Slice cake horizontally into 3 layers. Sandwich layers together with filling. Cover top and sides of cake with frosting. Arrange chocolate shavings over top. Sift mixed confectioners' sugar and cocoa over cake.

Makes 10 slices

CHOCOLATE RING CAKE

3 oz semisweet chocolate, broken into pieces
4 tablespoons unsalted butter
2–3 tablespoons strong coffee
3/4 cup superfine sugar
1 egg, separated, plus 1 extra egg white
1/2 teaspoon baking powder
1/3 cup heavy cream
1 1/4 cups all-purpose flour
1/2 teaspoon baking powder
CHOCOLATE FROSTING:
4 oz semisweet chocolate, broken into pieces
2/3 cup heavy cream
4 tablespoons butter
1 cup confectioners' sugar
few drops vanilla extract

TO DECORATE (Optional)
white chocolate leaves (page 9)
tiny edible flowers

Preheat oven to 350F (175C). Grease a 5-cup savarin or ring mold and dust with flour. In top of a double boiler or a bowl set over a saucepan of simmering water, melt chocolate with butter and coffee, stirring constantly until smooth. Add sugar and stir until sugar dissolves.

In a bowl, beat egg yolk, baking soda, and heavy cream, then stir into chocolate. Sift flour and baking powder into chocolate mixture and fold together.

In a medium-size bowl, whisk egg whites until stiff but not dry. Add 1 tablespoon to chocolate mixture, then pour chocolate mixture over egg whites and fold together. Pour into pan and bake 45–50 minutes, until set and spongy to touch. Let cool in the pan.

To make frosting: in a small saucepan, combine all ingredients and cook over very low heat, stirring constantly, until chocolate and butter have melted and are thoroughly combined.

Turn cake out onto a wire rack. Quickly pour frosting over cake and decorate with chocolate leaves and tiny flowers, if desired. Serve at once.

Serves 10

VARIATIONS: Omit decorations and sprinkle with 2 tablespoons toasted slivered almonds; the nuts give a crunchy texture. Omit frosting and serve with Dark Chocolate Sauce (page 87).

CHOCOLATE ALMOND TARTLETS

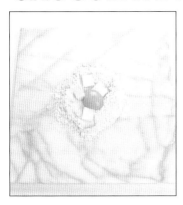

PÂTE SUCREE:
³/₈ cup all-purpose flour
2 tablespoons unsalted butter, softened
2 tablespoons superfine sugar
1 egg yolk
FILLING:
generous ¹/₄ cup packed brown sugar
2 tablespoons corn syrup
¹/₄ cup (2 oz) unsalted butter
1 cup slivered almonds, chopped and toasted
2 oz semisweet chocolate, melted (page 7)

Preheat oven to 375F (190C). To make pâte sucrée: sift flour onto a marble slab or cool surface. Make a well in the center.

Place butter, superfine sugar, and egg yolk in the center of well. Using the fingertips of one hand, work these ingredients together, then draw in the flour. Knead lightly until smooth, then let chill for 1 hour. On a lightly floured surface, roll out dough very thinly and use to line 12 tartlet pans. Prick bases and let chill 15 minutes. Press a square of foil into each tartlet shell and bake blind 8–10 minutes, until golden. Remove foil and place on wire rack to cool. To make filling, place brown sugar, syrup, butter, and 1 tablespoon water in a heavy saucepan.

Heat gently, stirring, until sugar has dissolved, then boil 5–7 minutes, until a little of the mixture, dropped into cold water, forms a soft ball; 240F (116C) on a sugar thermometer. Stir in all but 1 tablespoon of the almonds. Spoon filling into pastry shells before it starts to set. Finely chop reserved almonds. Spread melted chocolate over filling and sprinkle chopped nuts on edge of each tartlet to decorate.

Makes 10

STRAWBERRY CHOCOLATE TARTS

PIE DOUGH:
7 tablespoons butter, softened
2 teaspoons confectioners' sugar
1 egg yolk
1¹/₈ cups all-purpose flour
CHOCOLATE FILLING:
¹/₄ cup (2 oz) unsalted butter, softened
generous ¹/₄ cup superfine sugar
1 egg, beaten
2 oz semisweet chocolate, grated
¹/₂ cup ground almonds
TOPPING:
4 teaspoons red currant jelly
1 teaspoon kirsch
1¹/₂ cups strawberries, halved

To make dough: in a bowl, cream butter and confectioners' sugar together until soft and light. In another bowl, mix together egg yolk and 3 teaspoons water. Gradually stir into creamed mixture. Sift flour into mixture and mix to a smooth dough with a round-bladed knife. Wrap in plastic wrap and let chill for 1 hour. Preheat oven to 375F (190C). On a lightly floured surface, roll out dough thinly and use to line four 4-inch tartlet pans. To make filling: in a bowl, beat butter and superfine sugar until creamy, then beat in egg.

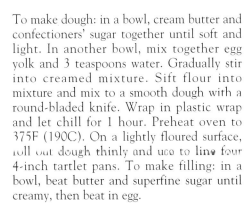

Stir in chocolate; add ground almonds and mix to a soft dropping consistency. Divide among pastry shells. Bake 20–25 minutes, until filling is set and pastry is crisp. To make topping: in a small saucepan, gently heat red currant jelly, stirring until completely dissolved. Stir in kirsch. Brush over chocolate tarts while still warm. Arrange strawberry halves on top and brush with remaining red currant jelly. Transfer to a wire rack to cool.

Makes 4

RUM TRUFFLE CAKE

7 oz semisweet chocolate, broken into pieces
1/2 cup unsalted butter
1/4 cup dark rum
3 eggs, separated
1/2 cup superfine sugar
3/4 cup all-purpose flour
1/2 cup ground almonds
FILLING & FROSTING:
7 oz semisweet chocolate
1 1/4 cups heavy cream
1 tablespoon dark rum
2 oz white chocolate, grated

Preheat oven to 350F (175C). Grease and flour a 2 1/2-inch deep 8-inch round cake pan. Line base with a circle of waxed paper. In a bowl set over a saucepan of simmering water, melt chocolate and butter, stirring occasionally, until smooth. Add rum and stir well.

Place egg yolks and sugar in a bowl set over a saucepan of simmering water. Whisk until thick and pale. Remove bowl from saucepan. Continue to whisk until mixture leaves a trail when whisk has been lifted. Stir chocolate mixture into egg yolk mixture until evenly blended. In a small bowl, mix flour and ground almonds. Add to chocolate mixture. Fold in carefully using a spatula.

In a bowl, whisk egg whites until stiff. Fold one-third at a time into chocolate mixture until all egg whites are incorporated. Pour batter into prepared pan. Bake 45–55 minutes, or until firm to touch in center. Turn out of pan and cool on wire rack.

To prepare filling, melt 4 oz of chocolate with 1/4 cup of heavy cream in a bowl set over a saucepan of simmering water. Stir in rum until well blended. Let stand until cool. To prepare frosting, whip 1/2 cup of heavy cream in a bowl until thick. Add half of rum-chocolate to whipped cream and fold in until smooth.

Cut cake in half. Sandwich together with frosting, spread remainder over top and sides. Chill cake and remaining rum-chocolate mixture in bowl. Melt remaining chocolate with heavy cream in bowl set over a saucepan of simmering water. Stir until smooth; let cool until thick. Spread chocolate mixture over cake to cover evenly. Shape rum-chocolate into 16 truffles. Coat in grated white chocolate. Arrange truffles on top of cake and chill set.

Serves 10

MISSISSIPPI MUD PIE

1 cup all-purpose flour
1/4 teaspoon baking powder
1 cup superfine sugar
1/2 cup (2 oz) butter
1 teaspoon vanilla extract
12 oz semisweet chocolate, coarsely chopped
2 small eggs, lightly beaten
TO SERVE:
good quality vanilla or coffee ice cream
Dark Chocolate Sauce (page 87)
1/2 cup chopped toasted pecans

Preheat oven to 325F (160C). Grease and line a 8-inch square cake pan. Mix together flour and baking powder. In a small saucepan, combine sugar, 3 tablespoons water, and butter. Bring to a boil and remove from heat. Stir in vanilla and half the chocolate and mix well until smooth. Let cool to room temperature.

Stir egg into cooled mixture and beat well. Add flour mixture and stir to blend. Fold in remaining chocolate. Pour into pan and bake 30–35 minutes, or until a skewer inserted into center of cake comes out clean. Let cool in pan 15 minutes. Carefully remove pie from pan onto plate. Cut into 8 squares and transfer to serving dishes. Top each with 1–2 scoops ice cream. Drizzle with warm chocolate sauce, sprinkle with pecans, and serve at once.

Serves 8

BANANA FUDGE CAKE

CAKE:
3/4 cup (6 oz) unsalted butter
1 1/8 cups packed brown sugar
3 eggs, beaten
3 ripe bananas
2 cups all-purpose flour
1/4 cup unsweetened cocoa
3 teaspoons baking powder
3 tablespoons milk
FROSTING:
2 oz semisweet chocolate, broken into pieces
1/4 cup (2 oz) unsalted butter
2 5/8 cups confectioners' sugar
1/4 cup light cream
chocolate shapes (page 11), to decorate

Preheat oven to 350F (180C). Grease and line two 8-inch round cake pans. In a bowl, cream together butter and brown sugar until light and fluffy. Gradually beat in eggs. Mash bananas or process in a blender or food processor until completely smooth. Stir into mixture. Sift flour, cocoa, and baking powder into a bowl. Gradually stir into creamed mixture, alternately with milk, to yield a fairly stiff dropping consistency. Divide mixture between prepared pans and bake 30 minutes, or until well risen and firm to the touch. Turn onto wire racks to cool.

To make frosting: in a saucepan, melt chocolate and butter together. Remove from heat and sift in half the confectioners' sugar; beat until smooth. Sift in remaining confectioners' sugar. Stir in cream and beat well until smooth and thick. Sandwich cakes together with one-quarter of frosting. Spread remaining frosting over top and sides of cake, swirling to make an attractive pattern. Decorate with chocolate triangles.

Serves 6–8

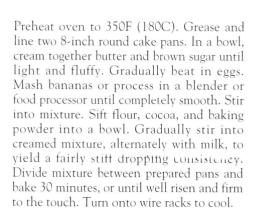

— DEVILS FOOD LAYER CAKE —

8 oz unsweetened chocolate, broken into pieces
8 oz cooked beets (not in vinegar)
$1/2$ cup (4 oz) unsalted butter, at room temperature
$2^1/2$ cups soft packed brown sugar
3 eggs
2 teaspoons vanilla extract
2 cups all-purpose flour
2 teaspoons baking powder
$1/2$ cup unsweetened cocoa
pinch of salt
$1/2$ cup buttermilk
FROSTING:
6 oz unsweetened or bittersweet chocolate
$3/4$ cup (6 oz) unsalted butter, softened
3 cups confectioners' sugar
6 tablespoons unsweetened cocoa
2 tablespoons milk

Preheat oven to 350F (180C). Grease and line base of 2 (8-inch) round cake pans with waxed paper. In a small bowl set over a saucepan of simmering water, melt chocolate until smooth. Let cool. Drain beets, reserving any juice. Place beets in a food processor and pulse until finely chopped. Add to reserved beet juice and set aside.

Beat butter, sugar, eggs, and vanilla on high speed for 5 minutes, scraping down bowl occasionally. Reduce speed to low and beat in melted chocolate. Stir together flour, baking powder, cocoa, and salt in medium-sized bowl.

With mixer on low, alternately beat in flour and buttermilk, starting and ending with flour. Mix until incorporated, about 1 minute. Add beets and juice and mix on medium speed until blended. The batter will be thin and pieces of beet will be visible in the batter. Divide batter equally between pans. Bake 40–45 minutes, or until a skewer inserted into center comes out clean. Let cool in pan 10 minutes, then invert onto wire racks. Let stand until cold.

Meanwhile, for the frosting, melt the chocolate. Then beat butter in a bowl until very soft and light colored. Sift confectioners' with cocoa and add to butter, about one-third at a time, alternating with milk. Mixture will be very thick. Now add cooled chocolate and mix together thoroughly; a rubber spatula is useful for this. If too thick to spread, add another 1–2 tablespoons milk until spreadable. If making mixture in advance do not chill.

To assemble, place a cake layer top-side down on serving plate. Spread with one-third of frosting and top with second layer, bottom side-up. Frost sides and top. Let stand at room temperature until set.

Serves 10–12

NOTE: the frosted cake may be held at room temperature, uncovered, overnight or chilled for up to 2 days. Bring to room temperature before serving.

– FLOURLESS CHOCOLATE CAKE –

7 oz bittersweet chocolate
3/4 cup (6 oz) butter, plus 2 tablespoons butter
4 eggs, separated
1 cup superfine sugar
TO DECORATE:
confectioners' sugar
unsweetened cocoa

Preheat oven to 375F (190C). Grease and line a 9-inch springform cake pan with waxed paper. In a bowl set over a saucepan of simmering water, melt chocolate and butter gently until smooth. Let cool slightly.

Beat egg yolks with half the sugar, until light and creamy. Fold in melted butter and chocolate mixture. Beat egg whites until stiff, add remaining sugar, and continue beating until stiff and glossy. Fold in remaining mixture.

Pour batter into pan and bake 40 minutes, or until a skewer comes out clean. Let cool on a wire rack. Serve warm or cold, dusted with confectioners' sugar and cocoa.

Serves 8–10

— SAUCY CHOCOLATE PUDDING —

3 oz each white chocolate, milk chocolate, semisweet
   chocolate
3 egg yolks
2 teaspoons finely grated grapefruit rind
2 teaspoons grapefruit juice
1 tablespoon ginger wine
1 tablespoon Southern Comfort liqueur
3/4 cup softened butter
2/3 cup heavy cream
3 tablespoons fromage frais
GRAPEFRUIT SAUCE:
finely grated rind and juice of 1 grapefruit
2 teaspoons cornstarch
1 tablespoon superfine sugar
TO DECORATE:
grapefruit slices and fresh mint sprigs

Break up each chocolate and place in separate bowls. Set each over a saucepan of simmering water. Stir occasionally until melted
and smooth. Stir an egg yolk into each. Stir
grapefruit rind and juice into white chocolate, ginger wine into milk chocolate, and
Southern Comfort into semisweet chocolate
until smooth. Let stand until cold. Beat
butter until light and fluffy. Whip cream
and fromage frais until thick. Add one-third
of each to chocolate mixtures and fold in
until smooth and evenly blended. Line 6
freezerproof molds with plastic wrap.

Divide milk chocolate mixture between
molds, making 1 layer. Repeat with white
and semisweet chocolate. Tap molds to
level and freeze until firm. To prepare sauce:
measure grapefruit juice, rind, and enough
water to measure 3/4 cup. Blend juice, cornstarch, and sugar. Bring to a boil, stirring
constantly. Cook gently 30 seconds, then
cool. Invert molds 20 minutes before
serving. Pour grapefruit juice around base.
Decorate with grapefruit slices and mint.

Serves 6

— RICH CHOCOLATE ICE CREAM —

2 eggs, plus 2 egg yolks
1/2 cup superfine sugar
1 1/4 cups light cream
8 oz semisweet chocolate, chopped
1 1/4 cups heavy cream
4 tablespoons dark rum

In a bowl, mix eggs, yolks, and sugar together.

In a saucepan, heat light cream and chocolate gently until chocolate has melted. Stir well to blend, then bring to a boil, stirring constantly. Pour onto egg mixture, stirring vigorously, then transfer to top of double boiler, or bowl placed over saucepan of boiling water. Cook, stirring constantly, until the custard is thick enough to coat the back of the spoon. Strain custard into a bowl and let cool.

In a bowl, whip heavy cream and rum together until stiff, then fold into cooled chocolate mixture. Pour into a rigid freezer-proof container, cover, seal, and freeze for 4 hours, or until firm. Scoop into chilled serving dishes to serve.

Serves 6–8

── CAROB & RAISIN ICE CREAM ──

2 cups skim milk
3 tablespoons sugar
3 teaspoons cornstarch
pinch of salt
3 egg yolks
$^2/_3$ cup semisweet carob chips
$^2/_3$ cup raisins
$^1/_2$ cup lowfat soft cheese
sweet cookies, to serve (optional)

In a saucepan, heat milk gently until almost boiling. In a bowl, blend sugar, cornstarch, salt, and eggs together, then gradually pour on milk, stirring constantly.

Pour mixture back into saucepan and heat gently until mixture thickens, stirring constantly. Bring to a boil and boil for 1 minute. In small bowl set over a saucepan of simmering water, melt carob chips. Add melted carob and raisins to custard, mixing well. Let cool. Gradually blend soft cheese into custard, mixing well. Pour into a chilled, shallow, rigid freezerproof container. Cover and freeze for $1^1/_2$–2 hours, or until mushy in consistency. Turn into a chilled bowl and beat with fork or whisk until smooth.

Return mixture to container, cover, and freeze for 1 hour. Beat mixture as before and return to container. Cover and freeze until firm. Transfer to refrigerator 30 minutes before serving to soften. Serve in glass dishes or glasses, with cookies, if desired.

Serves 6

— MOCHA ESPRESSO ICE CREAM —

2 cups milk
²/₃ cup heavy cream
generous ¹/₄ cup medium ground espresso coffee
3 oz semisweet chocolate, chopped
6 egg yolks
⁷/₈ cup superfine sugar
chocolate shavings, to decorate (optional)

In a saucepan, heat milk, cream, coffee, and 2 oz of the chocolate slowly until almost boiling. Remove from heat and set aside for 30 minutes to let flavors infuse.

In a large bowl, beat egg yolks and sugar together until thick and pale. Gradually beat in mocha mixture and transfer to a clean saucepan. Heat gently, stirring, until mixture thickens, but do not let boil. Let cool.

Transfer mixture to a rigid freezerproof container and freeze. Beat to mix and break up ice crystals after 1 hour. Repeat at hourly intervals until almost firm. Stir in remaining chocolate, cover, and let freeze completely. Remove from freezer 20 minutes before serving to let ice cream soften. Decorate with chocolate shavings, if desired.

Serves 4

ICED PRALINE RING

PRALINE:
generous ½ cup (4 oz) superfine sugar
generous ⅝ cup (4 oz) whole unblanched almonds
CHOCOLATE ICE CREAM:
6 oz semisweet chocolate, broken into pieces
⅔ cup (5 fl oz) light cream
1¼ cups (10 fl oz) heavy cream
2 tablespoons brandy
4 tablespoons heavy cream, whipped, to finish

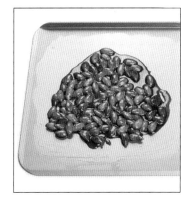

To make praline: in a heavy saucepan, heat sugar and almonds gently until sugar has melted. Increase heat and cook until almonds start to pop and turn brown, shaking saucepan to ensure almonds are evenly coated. Pour onto an oiled baking sheet and let stand until hardened. To make ice cream: in a saucepan, heat chocolate and light cream very gently until chocolate has melted, stirring until smooth. Let cool. In a bowl, whip heavy cream until soft peaks form, then carefully whisk in chocolate mixture and brandy. Do not overwhip.

Crush praline with rolling pin, or in food processor. Set a little aside for decoration, then fold remaining praline into chocolate mixture. Transfer to 3½-cup (1½-pint) ring mold, cover with foil, and freeze overnight. To serve, turn upside down over chilled plate and rub mold with a dishtowel wrung out in very hot water, until ice cream drops out. Pipe cream around top of ice cream and decorate with reserved praline. Cut into slices to serve.

Serves 8

-BOMBE AUX DEUX CHOCOLATS-

DARK CHOCOLATE ICE CREAM:
2 eggs, plus 2 egg yolks
generous ³/₈ cup superfine sugar
1¹/₄ cups light cream
8 oz semisweet chocolate, broken into pieces
1¹/₄ cups heavy cream
WHITE CHOCOLATE ICE CREAM:
5 oz white chocolate, broken into pieces
²/₃ cup milk
generous ¹/₄ cup superfine sugar
1¹/₄ cups heavy cream
chocolate caraque (page 9), to decorate

Place 6-cup bombe mold in freezer. In a bowl, beat together eggs, yolks, and sugar.

In a saucepan, heat light cream and semi-sweet chocolate gently until chocolate has melted. Bring to a boil, then add to egg mixture. Stir until smooth. Strain into a bowl and let cool. Whip heavy cream until thickened. Fold into chocolate mixture. Pour into a freezerproof container, cover, and freeze for 1 hour. Stir well, then refreeze until almost solid. Use to line bombe mold. Return to freezer. White chocolate ice cream: in a saucepan, heat white chocolate and half the milk, until milk is warm and chocolate melting.

Away from heat, stir until smooth, then set aside. In another saucepan, heat sugar and remaining milk. Let cool. Stir chocolate into sweetened milk. Whip cream until thickened and fold gently into chocolate. Fill center of bombe with white chocolate mixture. Cover and freeze until firm. To serve, dip mold into cold water. Turn out onto chilled serving dish and decorate with chocolate caraque.

Serves 6–8

CRÈME DE MENTHE BOMBES

3 egg yolks
generous ¹/₂ cup (4 oz) superfine sugar
1¹/₄ cups light cream
2 drops green food coloring
3 tablespoons crème de menthe
1¹/₄ cups heavy cream
4 oz after-dinner crisp chocolate mints, coarsely
  chopped
TO SERVE:
1 recipe Chocolate Sauce (page 86)
frosted mint leaves (below)

In a bowl, beat egg yolks and sugar together until creamy.

In a small saucepan, bring light cream to a boil, pour onto egg yolk mixture, and mix well. Transfer to double boiler or bowl set over a saucepan of boiling water and cook, stirring constantly, until thick enough to coat back of spoon. Strain into a bowl, stir in coloring and crème de menthe, and let cool. In a bowl, whip heavy cream, then whisk in mint custard. Pour into a rigid, freezerproof container, cover, and freeze for 3 hours, until half-set. Remove from freezer, stir well, and mix in chopped crisp chocolate mints.

Transfer to 6 (²/₃-cup) (5-fl oz) molds, cover with foil, and return to freezer until firm. To serve, dip mold into warm water to loosen ice cream and turn out onto chilled plate. Pour Chocolate Sauce around each bombe and decorate with frosted mint leaves.

Frosted Mint Leaves: brush the mint leaves with egg white, then dip in superfine sugar to coat. Leave on waxed paper for 1–2 hours to dry.

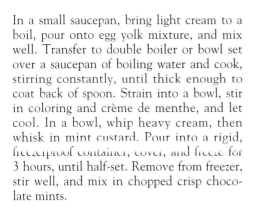

Serves 6

BLACK FOREST FONDUE

14 oz canned pitted black cherries
2/3 cup heavy cream
1 tablespoon kirsch
1 tablespoon cornstarch
CHOCOLATE CAKE:
2 eggs
1/2 cup (4 oz) butter, softened
generous 1/2 cup superfine sugar
3/4 cup self-rising flour
1/2 teaspoon baking powder
2 tablespoons unsweetened cocoa
1 tablespoon milk

Preheat oven to 375F (190C). Grease a 7-inch shallow, square cake pan.

To make cake: place eggs, butter, and sugar in a bowl. Sift flour, baking powder, and cocoa over. Add milk and beat together until smooth. Turn batter into pan and bake for 25 minutes, until cooked and firm to the touch. Turn onto a wire rack and let cool. Cut into small squares when cold.

Empty cherries and their juice into a blender or food processor and process until reasonably smooth. Transfer to a fondue pot, stir in cream, and heat until simmering. Add kirsch. In a small bowl, blend cornstarch and 1 tablespoon water together. Add to fondue pot and continue to cook, stirring, until mixture thickens. Transfer fondue pot to lighted spirit burner. Serve with chocolate cake to dip in.

Serves 4

– CLASSIC CHOCOLATE FONDUE –

9 oz semisweet chocolate
²/₃ cup heavy cream
2 tablespoons brandy
selection of fruit, such as strawberries, pineapple,
  banana, Cape gooseberries, figs, and kiwifruit, to
  serve
SPONGE FINGERS:
scant ¹/₄ cup superfine sugar
1 egg
scant ¹/₄ cup all-purpose flour, sifted

Preheat oven to 375F (190C). Line a baking
sheet with nonstick paper.

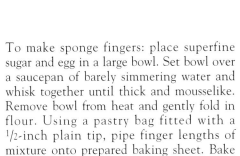

To make sponge fingers: place superfine
sugar and egg in a large bowl. Set bowl over
a saucepan of barely simmering water and
whisk together until thick and mousselike.
Remove bowl from heat and gently fold in
flour. Using a pastry bag fitted with a
¹/₂-inch plain tip, pipe finger lengths of
mixture onto prepared baking sheet. Bake
6–8 minutes, until golden.

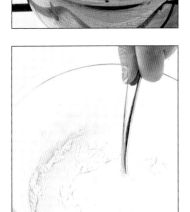

Transfer sponge fingers to wire rack to cool.
Break up chocolate and place in fondue pot
with cream and brandy. Heat gently, stirring, until chocolate has melted and
mixture is smooth. Transfer fondue pot to
lighted spirit burner and serve with sponge
fingers and fruit.

Serves 4–6

VARIATION: for children, substitute
orange juice for brandy.

— CHOCOLATE HONEY FONDUE —

10 oz semisweet chocolate
1 heaping tablespoon honey
1 1/4 cups heavy cream
SPICED FRUIT:
2 2/3 cups no-soak dried fruit, such as apricots and
    prunes
1 cinnamon stick
1 star anise
4 cloves
1 tablespoon honey

To prepare fruit: place in a saucepan and cover with water. Add cinnamon stick, star anise, and cloves. Bring to a boil.

Stir in honey and remove from heat. Set aside and let stand until cold. Drain fruit and pat dry on paper towels. Arrange on 6 serving plates.

Break up chocolate and place in fondue pot with honey and cream. Heat gently, stirring until chocolate has melted and mixture is smooth. Transfer fondue pot to lighted spirit burner and serve with fruit.

Serves 6

NOTE: choose a fragrant blossom honey such as Mexican wildflower honey for both fondue and fruit.

—— CHOCOLATE BROWNIES ——

³/₈ cup all-purpose flour
generous ¹/₄ cup unsweetened cocoa
¹/₂ cup (4 oz) butter
generous 1 cup superfine sugar
few drops vanilla extract
2 eggs, beaten
generous ³/₈ cup chopped walnuts
FROSTING:
4 oz semisweet chocolate, broken into pieces
²/₃ cup thick sour cream

Preheat oven to 325F (160C). Grease an 8-inch square cake pan. Sift flour and cocoa onto a plate.

Place butter, sugar, and 3 teaspoons cold water into a saucepan. Stir over low heat to melt butter. Remove from heat; stir in vanilla extract, then beat in eggs, one at a time. Add flour and cocoa; beat to a smooth shiny mixture. Stir in walnuts. Pour batter into pan. Bake for 20 minutes, until set. Let cool in pan.

To make frosting: in a bowl set over a saucepan of simmering water, melt chocolate, stirring until smooth. Remove from the heat. Stir in sour cream; beat until evenly blended. Spoon topping over brownies and make a swirling pattern with a palette knife. Let set in a cool place. Cut into squares and remove from pan.

Makes 9 large or 16 small brownies

MINI CHOCOLATE LOGS

3 eggs
2 tablespoons plus 2 teaspoons superfine sugar
1/4 cup all-purpose flour
1 tablespoon unsweetened cocoa
confectioners' sugar (optional)
FILLING:
1 1/4 cups heavy cream
4 oz semisweet chocolate, broken into pieces
TO DECORATE:
marzipan toadstools & holly sprigs

Preheat oven to 400F (200C). Then line a 1-inch deep 12-inch baking sheet with waxed paper.

In a bowl set over a saucepan of simmering water, whisk eggs and sugar until thick and pale. Remove bowl from saucepan, continue whisking until mixture leaves a trail. Sift in flour and cocoa, fold in until evenly blended. Pour onto baking sheet. Spread to edges. Bake 8–10 minutes, or until firm to touch. Cool for a few minutes and remove cake. Remove waxed paper, trim edges, and cut cake in half. To prepare filling: in a bowl set over a saucepan of simmering water, melt 1/4 cup heavy cream and chocolate, stirring occasionally, until melted.

Whip remaining cream until almost thick. When chocolate has cooled, fold into whipped cream. Using one-third of chocolate cream, spread evenly over each cake. Roll each in a firm roll from long edge. Wrap in plastic wrap and chill 20 minutes, or until firm. Cut each roll in 6 lengths. Spread with remaining chocolate cream using a palette knife; mark cream in lines. Sprinkle with confectioners' sugar, if desired. Decorate, then chill until served.

Serves 12

– CHOCOLATE CHECKERBOARDS –

¾ cup (6 oz) butter
generous ¾ cup superfine sugar
few drops vanilla extract
2 eggs
1 lb 2 oz all-purpose flour
2 teaspoons baking powder
1 teaspoon milk
6 teaspoons unsweetened cocoa

Grease several baking sheets. Divide butter and sugar evenly between 2 bowls.

To make vanilla dough: beat one half of butter and sugar until light and fluffy. Beat in vanilla extract and 1 egg. Sift half flour and 1 teaspoon baking powder into bowl. Blend in with spoon, then work by hand to form a soft dough. Make chocolate dough in same way with remaining butter, sugar and egg, adding milk and sifting cocoa in with remaining flour and baking powder. Divide each portion of dough into 4 equal pieces.

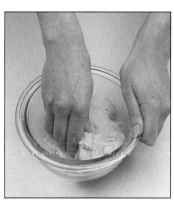

On a floured surface, roll each piece into a rope 12 inches long. Place a chocolate rope next to a vanilla one. Place a chocolate one on top of the vanilla one and a vanilla one on top of the chocolate. Press firmly together to from a square. Wrap in plastic wrap. Repeat with remaining dough. Chill for 1 hour. Preheat oven to 350F (180C). Cut dough into 48 slices and place on baking sheets. Bake 20 minutes, until cookies are lightly browned.

Makes 48

– DOUBLE CHOCOLATE COOKIES –

¹/₂ cup (4 oz) butter
generous ¹/₄ cup granulated sugar
generous ¹/₄ cup soft packed brown sugar
1 egg, beaten
few drops vanilla extract
scant 1 cup all-purpose flour
2 tablespoons unsweetened cocoa
¹/₂ teaspoon baking soda
³/₄ cup white chocolate chips

Preheat oven to 350F (180C). Grease several baking sheets.

In a bowl, beat butter with granulated and soft brown sugars until creamy. Gradually add egg and vanilla extract. Sift flour, cocoa, and baking soda into a bowl. Mix well, then stir in chocolate chips.

Drop teaspoonfuls of mixture, spaced apart, onto baking sheets. Bake 10–12 minutes, until firm. Let cool on baking sheets for a few minutes, then let cool completely on wire racks.

Makes about 48

FLORENTINES

¹/₄ cup (2 oz) unsalted butter
¹/₃ cup heavy cream
generous ¹/₃ cup superfine sugar
finely grated rind 1 lemon
1 teaspoon lemon juice
³/₈ cup all-purpose flour, sifted
³/₄ cup slivered blanched almonds
²/₃ cup chopped mixed candied citrus peel
²/₃ cup chopped candied cherries
2 tablespoons golden raisins
2 tablespoons chopped angelica
TO FINISH:
3 oz semisweet chocolate, chopped
3 oz white chocolate, chopped

Preheat oven to 350F (180C). Grease several baking sheets. Line with nonstick paper. Place butter, cream, sugar, lemon rind, and juice in a large saucepan and stir over medium heat until melted. Remove from heat and stir in flour, almonds, mixed peel, cherries, golden raisins, and angelica. Drop teaspoonfuls of mixture onto baking sheets, spaced well apart. Using a fork dipped in cold water, flatten each round to a circle about 2¹/₂ inches in diameter.

Bake 10–12 minutes, until lightly browned around edges. Cool on baking sheets for a few minutes, then remove with a palette knife and place on wire racks to cool completely. Melt semisweet and white chocolate in bowls placed over saucepans of simmering water. Spread flat sides of half the florentines with semisweet chocolate, and remainder with white chocolate. Using a fork, mark chocolate into wavy lines. Let set with chocolate uppermost.

Makes 28

– PECAN & CHOC-CHIP COOKIES –

¹/₂ cup (4 oz) unsalted butter
generous ¹/₄ cup granulated sugar
generous ¹/₄ cup brown sugar
1 egg
few drops vanilla extract
³/₄ cup all-purpose flour
2 tablespoons unsweetened cocoa
¹/₂ teaspoon baking soda
4 oz semisweet chocolate chips
scant ³/₈ cup pecan nuts, coarsely chopped

Preheat oven to 350F (180C). Grease 2–3 baking sheets.

In a bowl, cream butter and sugars together until light and fluffy. In another bowl, beat egg and vanilla extract together; gradually beat into creamed mixture. Sift flour, cocoa, and baking soda over creamed mixture. Stir in carefully. Stir in chocolate chips and pecan nuts. Drop teaspoons of mixture, well apart, on baking sheets and bake 10–15 minutes, or until mixture has spread and cookies are starting to feel firm. Carefully transfer to wire racks to cool and become crisp. Store in an airtight container.

Makes about 28

VARIATIONS:
Vanilla Chocolate Chip Cookies: omit cocoa and add extra 6 teaspoons flour.
Mocha Chocolate Chop Cookies: add 2 teaspoons instant coffee granules with flour and cocoa.
Fruit & Chocolate Chip Cookies: replace nuts with chopped dried apricots, pineapple, and coconut flakes.

— CRÈME DE MENTHE COOKIES —

8 oz semisweet chocolate, broken into pieces
6 teaspoons butter
1¾ cups digestive cookie crumbs
¾ cup plain cake crumbs
superfine sugar, for sprinkling
FILLING:
¼ cup (2 oz) unsalted butter
1 cup confectioners' sugar, sifted
2 teaspoons crème de menthe

Prepare filling first. In a bowl, beat butter with a wooden spoon until soft and smooth. Gradually beat in confectioners' sugar and crème de menthe until light and fluffy.

In a bowl set over a saucepan of simmering water, heat chocolate and butter, stirring occasionally until melted. Add cookie and cake crumbs and stir until evenly mixed and mixture forms a ball. Sprinkle a 10-inch square of foil with superfine sugar.

Roll out chocolate mixture on the foil to an 8-inch square. Spread crème de menthe mixture evenly over chocolate square to within ½ inch of edges. Roll up carefully into a neat roll using the foil to help. Wrap in foil and chill until firm. Cut into thin slices as and when required.

Makes 20 slices

CHOCOLATE BALLS

$^1/_2$ cup (4 oz) butter
3 tablespoons corn syrup
4 oz semisweet chocolate, broken into pieces
$^1/_2$ cup no-soak dried apricots, chopped
1 cup muesli-style cereal
drinking chocolate powder

Place butter and corn syrup in a saucepan and heat gently until melted.

Add chocolate to saucepan and let melt. Beat together until smooth, then add apricots and muesli. Mix well. When cool, let chill for 1 hour.

Take teaspoons of mixture and roll into balls. Toss in drinking chocolate, then place in petit fours cases. Let chill until firm.

Makes about 20

CHOCOLATE FINGERS

2 egg whites
$^{1}/_{2}$ cup superfine sugar
generous $^{1}/_{3}$ cup all-purpose flour
2 teaspoons unsweetened cocoa
$^{1}/_{4}$ cup (2 oz) unsalted butter, melted
2 oz white chocolate, melted

Preheat oven to 400F (200C). Line 2 baking sheets with nonstick paper. Place egg whites in a bowl and whisk until stiff. Add superfine sugar gradually, whisking well after each addition. Sift flour and cocoa over surface of mixture, add butter, and fold in carefully until mixture is evenly blended.

Place 3 spoonfuls of mixture onto each baking sheet, well spaced apart. Spread each into a thin circle. Bake, one sheet at a time, 3–4 minutes. Loosen each circle with a palette knife, then return to the oven for 1 minute.

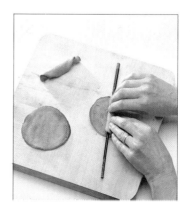

Take out one chocolate circle at a time and quickly roll around a greased chopstick, or wooden spoon handle, to form a tube. Slip off and cool on wire rack. Repeat with remaining circles. Cook second sheet of mixture, then repeat to make about 25 fingers. Dip both ends of each finger into melted chocolate. Let set on a paper-lined baking sheet. Store in an airtight container until required.

Makes 25

── CHOCOLATE TRUFFLE CUPS ──

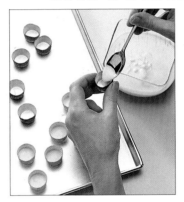

1 lb white chocolate, broken into pieces
¹/₄ cup (2 oz) unsalted butter, softened
6 teaspoons heavy cream
4 teaspoons cherry brandy
pink, green, and yellow food colorings
4 teaspoons Chartreuse
4 teaspoons apricot brandy
6 pistachios, chopped

In a bowl set over a saucepan of simmering water, melt chocolate, stirring occasionally until smooth. Remove bowl from saucepan and let cool. Place 36 foil cases on a baking sheet; spoon a little chocolate into each.

Using a fine brush, coat inside of each case; let set. Add butter and cream to remaining chocolate, stir until smooth. Divide mixture between 3 bowls. Flavor one with cherry brandy and tint pink, flavor another with Chartreuse and tint green, and other with apricot brandy and tint with yellow and pink coloring to give an apricot color.

When chocolate mixtures are set enough to peak softly, place each in a separate pastry bag fitted with a small star tip, pipe swirls of each flavor into 12 chocolate cases. Sprinkle with pistachios and let set. Pack in pretty containers.

Makes 36

CREAM TRUFFLES

¹/₃ cup heavy cream
1 vanilla bean
2 tablespoons superfine sugar
1 egg yolk
5 oz semisweet chocolate, broken into pieces
2 tablespoons unsalted butter, softened
2 teaspoons crème de cacao or brandy, rum, or other
  liqueurs, such as Tia Maria
COATING:
4 teaspoons unsweetened cocoa
2 teaspoons confectioners' sugar

Line a jelly roll pan with nonstick paper. In a saucepan, bring cream almost to a boil with vanilla bean. Remove from heat, cover, and set aside 30 minutes. Remove vanilla bean. In a bowl, whisk together superfine sugar and egg yolk until pale and thick; whisk into cream in saucepan. Return saucepan to heat and heat gently without boiling. Add chocolate and butter, stirring until smooth. Stir in crème de cacao. Pour into pan and let chill 1 hour, or until firm.

To make coating: sift cocoa and confectioners' sugar together onto a plate. Pull off small pieces of chilled truffle mixture and roll into balls. Roll each ball in sifted cocoa mixture and place in paper candy cases. Store in refrigerator and eat within 2-3 days.

Makes 20

NOTE: as an alternative truffles may be coated in melted semisweet or white chocolate, or rolled in crushed praline.

— CLASSIC CHOCOLATE FUDGE —

1¹/₄ cups heavy cream
¹/₄ cup milk
2 cups superfine sugar
3 tablespoons light corn syrup
¹/₈ teaspoon salt
6 oz unsweetened or bittersweet chocolate, chopped
2 tablespoons unsalted butter
¹/₂ teaspoon vanilla extract

Lightly grease an 8-inch square cake pan. In a large, heavy saucepan, gently heat cream and milk until steaming. Remove from heat and add sugar, corn syrup, and salt. Stir until sugar has dissolved.

Stir in chocolate until melted. Return saucepan to medium-high heat. Bring to a boil and cook, covered, 2–3 minutes, until steam washes any sugar crystals down from sides of saucepan. Uncover, reduce heat to medium, and cook for 10 minutes, without stirring, until mixture reaches soft-ball stage, or 238F (119C) on a candy thermometer. Remove from heat and cool the bottom of saucepan in a bowl of cold water. When bubbling stops, add butter, and vanilla, but do not stir. Leave until fudge reaches 110F (43C).

Beat with wooden spoon until fudge starts to lose its gloss. Spoon fudge into pan and let stand at room temperature until cool but not firm. Cut into 1-inch squares before it sets. The fudge may need to set overnight depending upon the temperature indoors.

Makes ³/₄ lb

VANILLA SWIRL FUDGE

¹/₂ recipe Classic Chocolate Fudge (see opposite)
³/₄ cup heavy cream
1 cup superfine sugar
¹/₄ cup (2 oz) butter
2 teaspoons light corn syrup
1 teaspoon vanilla extract

Lightly grease a 8-inch square cake pan. Follow the instructions for chocolate fudge in one saucepan, while at same time cooking vanilla fudge (below).

In a saucepan, combine heavy cream, sugar, butter, and corn syrup over low heat. Stir constantly with a wooden spoon until sugar dissolves and butter is melted. Wash down sides of saucepan with pastry brush dipped in water to dissolve sugar crystals. Bring mixture to a boil and cook until it reaches soft ball stage, or 238F (119C) on a candy thermometer. Remove pan from heat and stop cooking by plunging bottom of saucepan in a bowl of cold water for 1 minute. Add vanilla, but do not stir.

When thermometer reads 110F (43C), mix each saucepan of fudge with a wooden spoon until it starts to lose its gloss. Place alternate spoonfuls of chocolate and vanilla fudge into prepared pan and using handle of clean wooden spoon, swirl mixture together until marbled. Let stand until cool but not yet firm, then cut into squares. Leave until set (which may take overnight, depending upon the room temperature indoors).

Makes ³/₄ lb

— CHOCOLATE DECORATIONS —

4 oz semisweet chocolate, broken into pieces
8 oz white chocolate, broken into pieces
pink, green, and yellow oil-based, or powdered food
  colorings
pink, green, and yellow ribbon

Place chocolate in separate bowls set over saucepans of simmering water. Stir occasionally until melted. Divide half white chocolate between 3 bowls and color pink, green, and yellow with food colorings.

To make novelty shapes, draw around cookie cutters on nonstick paper. Invert paper and place on a baking sheet. Half-fill 2 waxed paper pastry bags with melted semisweet chocolate. Snip a small point off one bag and pipe a fine outline of chocolate into shapes to give an overfilled and rounded appearance.

Repeat to make different shaped chocolate decorations, using white and colored chocolate. Let set hard, then carefully peel off paper, taking care not to mark surfaces. Sandwich matching shapes together with remaining melted chocolates, placing ribbon loops in-between. Decorate shapes with piped colored chocolate using a waxed paper pastry bag. Let decorations dry before hanging up with different color ribbons.

Makes about 20

— HAND-DIPPED CHOCOLATES —

3 oz ready-to-roll fondant icing
rose and violet flavorings
pink and mauve food colorings
2 oz white marzipan
6 maraschino cherries
6 crème de menthe cherries
6 Brazil nuts
6 whole almonds
6 oz semisweet chocolate, broken into pieces
6 oz white chocolate, broken into pieces
6 oz milk chocolate, broken into pieces
crystallized rose and violet petals

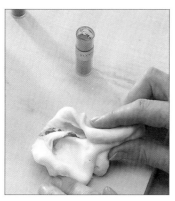

Cut fondant into 2 pieces: flavor half with rose flavorings and color pale pink.

Flavor remaining piece with violet flavoring and color pale mauve. Roll out fondant to 1/2 inch thickness and cut into shapes using cocktail cutters. Place on a nonstick paper-lined baking sheet. Shape marzipan into various shapes by rolling bite-size pieces between hands into balls, logs, or ovals. Arrange on baking sheet. Let dry for several hours or overnight. Pat cherries dry. Toast nuts until golden brown.

Melt each type of chocolate in separate bowls set over simmering water and stir until melted. Using a fork, dip one prepared center at a time into chocolate; tap to remove excess, and place chocolate on a paper-lined baking sheet. Leave plain, or mark top with a fork or with piped choco-late. Decorate rose and violet centers with crystallized petals. Continue to dip all centers, giving a variety of white, semisweet, or milk chocolate.

Makes about 30

CHOCOLATE SAUCE

4 oz semisweet chocolate
1 1/4 cups milk
vanilla extract, to taste
1 teaspoon sugar
4 egg yolks, well beaten, room temperature

Chop or cut chocolate into pieces.

In a heavy-bottom, small saucepan, heat milk, chocolate, vanilla extract, and sugar over low heat until chocolate melts, stirring constantly. When liquid is just bubbling round edge of saucepan, remove from heat. Spoon a small amount of the hot liquid into egg yolks. Add yolks to chocolate. Return to heat and continue stirring for 2–3 minutes without simmering, until thickened.

Serve hot with poached pears, ice cream, steamed puddings, or soufflés.

Makes about 1 1/2 cups

—— DARK CHOCOLATE SAUCE ——

6 oz semisweet chocolate, broken into pieces
1/2 cup strong coffee or water
1/4 cup superfine sugar

Place chocolate in top of double boiler or bowl set over a saucepan of simmering water. Add coffee and sugar.

Stir over medium heat until chocolate melts and sauce is smooth and creamy. Serve hot or cold.

Serves 4–6

NOTE: serve with Two Chocolate Terrine (pages 32-33), if desired.

BITTER MOCHA SAUCE

3 oz semisweet chocolate, broken into pieces
1 tablespoon dark very strong coarsely ground
   expresso coffee
1 1/4 cups heavy cream
1 1/2 teaspoons butter

Place chocolate in top of double boiler or
bowl and set aside. In a saucepan, combine
coffee and heavy cream. Bring to a boil and
remove from heat. Let infuse 30 minutes.

Strain coffee and cream mixture through a
fine strainer into the chocolate. Place over a
saucepan of simmering water and stir until
chocolate melts.

Whisk in butter to make sauce glossy and
serve at once.

Serves 6–8

BRANDY ALEXANDER

3 ice cubes, cracked
$^1/_2$ measure cream
$^1/_2$ measure brandy
$^1/_2$ measure Tia Maria or crème de cacao
1 chocolate stick, to serve
TO DECORATE:
beaten egg white, or lemon or lime wedge
finely grated or chopped semisweet chocolate, or
   unsweetened cocoa mixed with superfine sugar, or
   ground coffee beans

Frost a cocktail glass with grated or chopped chocolate, or cocoa mixed with superfine sugar, or coffee.

Place cracked ice cubes into a cocktail shaker or screw-top jar. Pour the cream, brandy, and Tia Maria into shaker or jar; shake to mix. Strain drink into glass. Add the chocolate stick and serve.

NOTE: To frost the glass wipe the rim with a lemon or lime wedge, or dip it into lightly beaten egg white. Ensure the glass is held upside down by the stem to prevent the juice running down the bowl of the glass. Put a layer of the desired frosting on a saucer, then dip the glass rim in until evenly coated. For extra effect, sugar can be colored with edible food coloring. If using coffee use only powdered instant or finely ground coffee beans, do not use granular coffee.

Serves 1

FOXY LADY

3 ice cubes, cracked
1 measure Amaretto di Saronno or almond liqueur
$1/2$ measure Tia Maria or crème de cacao
1 measure heavy cream
TO DECORATE:
lightly beaten egg white
finely grated or chopped semisweet chocolate, or
  unsweetened cocoa mixed with a little superfine
  sugar
chocolate dragée

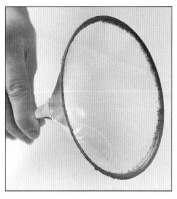

Frost rim of a cocktail glass with egg white and semisweet chocolate, or cocoa mixed with superfine sugar (see page 89).

Place ice in a cocktail shaker or screw-top jar. Pour Amaretto and Tia Maria into shaker or jar; add cream. Shake to mix drink. Strain into glass. Top with dragée or finely grated or chopped chocolate.

Serves 1

VELVET GLOVE

4 ice cubes, cracked
1 measure Kahlua or Tia Maria
½ measure Amaretto di Saronno or almond liqueur
1 measure heavy cream
TO DECORATE:
lightly beaten egg white
ground coffee beans or instant coffee
finely grated or chopped chocolate (optional)

Frost rim of a small brandy balloon glass with egg white and ground coffee or instant coffee (see page 89). Place half the cracked ice cubes in a cocktail shaker or screw-top jar. Place remaining ice into glass.

Pour Kahlua and Amaretto into shaker or jar; add cream. Shake to mix and strain into glass. Top with ground coffee, or finely grated or chopped chocolate, if desired.

Serves 1

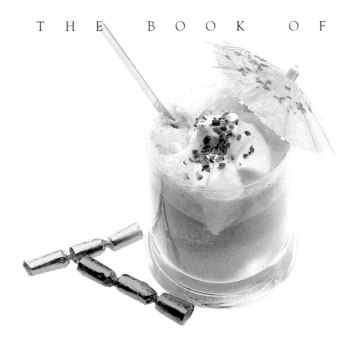

SNOWBALL FIZZ

4 oz white chocolate
finely grated rind and juice 2 limes
1½ cups red or white grape juice
1 egg white
1 tablespoon plus 2 teaspoons superfine sugar
soda or sparkling water
1 teaspoon grated milk chocolate
TO SERVE:
4 drinking straws
4 cocktail umbrellas (optional)

Break up white chocolate. Place in bowl set over a saucepan of simmering water. Stir occasionally until melted and smooth. Stir in lime rind and juice until well blended. Divide grape juice equally among 4 glasses. Add a quarter of chocolate-lime mixture to each and stir until well blended.

In a bowl, whisk egg white until stiff. Add sugar a little at a time and whisk until thick. Just before serving, divide meringue among glasses and fill to top with soda or sparkling water. Sprinkle with milk chocolate and serve with straws and cocktail umbrellas, if desired.

Serves 4

MALTED MILKSHAKE

14½ oz canned evaporated milk
2 cups chilled milk
3 tablespoons unsweetened cocoa
2 teaspoons brown sugar
3 tablespoons malt extract
8 scoops vanilla ice cream
4 chocolate flakes

Place 4 glass tumblers in the refrigerator to chill for 30 minutes.

Depending on the size of blender available, either blend in 1 or 2 batches. Place the milks, cocoa, sugar, malt extract, and half the ice cream into a pitcher or blender and blend for 2 minutes, until frothy.

Pour into chilled glasses, top each drink with a scoop of ice cream, and a chocolate flake. Serve.

Serves 4

VARIATION: Use powdered malted chocolate drink instead of cocoa, if preferred, and reduce the amount of sugar.

SPANISH HOT CHOCOLATE

3 oz semisweet chocolate, broken into pieces
2 cups milk
TO DECORATE:
cinnamon sticks
orange zest

Place chocolate in top of a double boiler or a bowl placed over a saucepan of simmering water and heat until melted. In a saucepan, heat milk to a boil. Using a wooden spoon, slowly stir a little boiling milk into the chocolate.

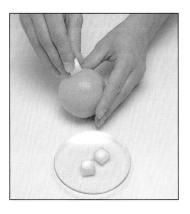

Using a wire whisk, whisk in remaining milk and continue to whisk until mixture is frothy. Pour into heatproof glasses or cups and decorate with cinnamon sticks and orange zest.

Serves 2

VARIATION: Rub sugar lumps over a whole orange to remove the zest, then add the sugar to the hot chocolate.

CHOCOLATE MILK FLOAT

1¹/₄ cups superfine sugar
scant 1 cup unsweetened cocoa
TO SERVE:
milk (see below)
vanilla ice cream
whipped cream
sifted unsweetened cocoa, for sprinkling

In a saucepan, heat sugar with 1¹/₄ cups water until sugar has dissolved. Bring to a boil and boil for 3 minutes, stirring occasionally. Whisk in cocoa and continue whisking over medium heat until smooth. Let cool, then keep syrup in refrigerator until required. For each Chocolate Milk Float serving: whisk together 1 cup milk and 9 teaspoons chilled chocolate syrup.

Pour into a chilled glass, float a scoop of ice cream on the chocolate milk, and top with a generous spoonful of whipped cream. Sprinkle with a little cocoa and serve at once.

Makes 1¹/₂ cups syrup

NOTE: the syrup can be kept in the refrigerator for several weeks and used as required. This also makes an excellent topping for ice cream.

INDEX